itsu

eat beautiful

20-minute
suppers

itsu

eat beautiful

Julian Metcalfe & Blanche Vaughan

MITCHELL BEAZLEY

20-minute suppers

quick, simple & delicious
noodles, grains, rice & soups

An Hachette UK Company
www.hachette.co.uk

First published in Great Britain in 2016 by Mitchell Beazley,
a division of Octopus Publishing Group Ltd, Carmelite House,
50 Victoria Embankment, London EC4Y 0DZ
www.octopusbooks.co.uk
www.octopusbooksusa.com

Distributed in the US by Hachette Book Group, 1290 Avenue of the
Americas, 4th and 5th Floors, New York, NY 10020

Distributed in Canada by Canadian Manda Group, 664 Annette St,
Toronto, Ontario, Canada M6S 2C8

ISBN 978-1-78472-130-5

A CIP catalogue record for this book is available from the
British Library.

Notes: This book contains some dishes made with raw or lightly
cooked eggs. It is prudent for more vulnerable people, such as
pregnant and nursing mothers, people with weakened immune
systems, the elderly, babies and young children, to avoid dishes
made with uncooked or lightly cooked eggs.

Unless stated otherwise in the recipes:
- All calorie counts and fat content figures are per serving.
- All spoon measures are level.
- All eggs are medium.
- All vegetables should be peeled, as necessary.
- All herbs and leaves should be washed and trimmed, as necessary.
- Chillies can be used with or without seeds, depending on how spicy
  you like your food.
- Standard bunches of herbs are 20g (¾oz), small bunches are 10g
  (¼oz), and large bunches are 30g (1oz).

Photographer: Tamin Jones
Food Stylist: Annie Rigg
Props Stylist: Liz Belton
Designed by Grade Design
Illustrator: Mark McConnell
Nutritional Consultant: Angela Dowden
Copy Editor: Jo Richardson

Publisher: Alison Starling
Art Director: Yasia Williams-Leedham
Senior Editor: Leanne Bryan
Production Manager: Katherine Hockley

Julian Metcalfe, co-founder of
Pret A Manger and pioneer of natural
food, is on to his next crusade: itsu …
revolutionising affordable, healthy food.

Years of listening to customers
persuaded him to build a new type
of food place altogether: light, green
and good for you.

itsu's EAT BEAUTIFUL menu celebrates
the amazing flavours of the Far East;
high in nutrients yet refreshingly low
in calories and saturated fat. With
protein-packed, low-carb salads,
brown rice dishes, freshly made sushi,
soups and noodles – this is fresh food
that tastes as good as it looks.

Blanche Vaughan is a food writer
and chef who worked at the River
Cafe, Moro and St John. She
has written for the *Guardian* and
published four books with Weidenfeld
& Nicolson including In *One Pot* and
Egg. She wrote *itsu: the cookbook*
with Julian Metcalfe.

Contents

Introduction

Welcome to our second cookbook, *itsu 20-minute suppers*.

The itsu crusade brings lively, healthy Asian food to the home and the high street in an uncomplicated manner. Our EAT BEAUTIFUL ethos celebrates the amazing flavours of the Far East while being high in nutrients yet refreshingly low in calories and saturated fat. And we favour simple-to-follow recipes using easy-to-get-hold-of ingredients.

Once again our chefs have teamed up with the brilliant Blanche Vaughan to provide some of the dishes we offer in itsu, as well as new ideas for noodles, grains, rice and soups.

To make things easy, Blanche and the team have created recipes using ingredients that are available from the convenience stores and mini-markets to be found all over our towns and cities, which continue to improve in the variety and quality of the products they offer.

In harmony with our shops, restaurants and cafés, itsu recipes are for everyday healthy living… big on flavour yet free of stress to shop for and cook. Being busy should be no barrier to cooking light, delicious food every night of the week.

Julian Metcalfe

Founder of itsu, co-founder of Pret A Manger

Ingredients kit

These useful ingredients are worth stocking up on as they appear in most of the recipes in the book, and the condiments and other seasonings will add immediate flavour to dishes.

In the storecupboard
soy sauce
fish sauce
hot chilli sauces, such as itsu Hot•su
    Potsu Sauce and Sriracha chilli sauce
mirin
sesame paste or tahini
spices: ground turmeric, ground
    cinnamon, ground cumin, whole
    star anise
chilli flakes
garlic paste
ginger paste
Shaoxing wine
rice vinegar

toasted sesame oil
agave syrup
dried and ready-cooked noodles
    (*see* pages 16–19]
ready-cooked rice (*see* pages 84–85)
canned lentils
ready-cooked grains (*see* pages 86–87)

In the fridge
fresh root ginger
hot red and green chillies
garlic bulb
fresh herbs: coriander, parsley, basil,
    chives and mint

In the freezer
lemon grass stalks
ready-made chicken stock (*see* page 180)
ready-chopped herbs: coriander,
    parsley, chives, mint

Alternative ingredients

We all know how frustrating it is when you get to the shop and certain ingredients on your list are unavailable. However, this can be a great opportunity to try out alternative options within the same ingredient category – and make the recipe your own! Here are some helpful ideas for substitutions to ensure that your quick shopping trip provides everything you need for your meal. It is worth taking a photo of these different ingredients as a visual reminder, so that you never get stuck for ideas.

Chillies

hot red and green chillies – deseed, partially deseed or leave all the seeds in to vary the heat

chilli sauces

chilli flakes

whole dried red chillies

chilli pastes

Oils

coconut oil – good for flavour, but don't use in a wok as it burns easily

groundnut oil – made with peanuts, so watch out for allergies; great for frying as it can be heated to high temperatures without burning

olive oil

ghee – gives a delicious, rich background flavour

vegetable oil – often made with rapeseed; very light in flavour and great for frying

nut oils, such as walnut or hazelnut

Greens
These can be interchanged in all the recipes, though the coarser-textured varieties will have a longer cooking time

curly kale – takes a few minutes longer than spinach to cook, but turns wonderfully crisp when stir-fried

Chinese cabbage

tatsoi

spinach

chard

choi sum

cavolo nero

spring greens

pak choi

white and red cabbage

rocket and watercress – can be cooked like spinach for a peppery flavour

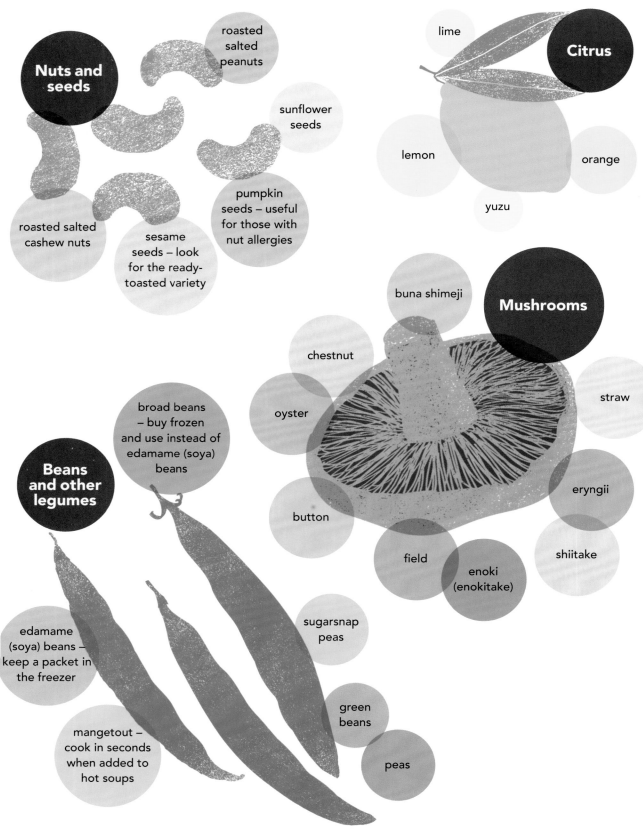

Nuts and seeds

roasted salted peanuts

sunflower seeds

roasted salted cashew nuts

sesame seeds – look for the ready-toasted variety

pumpkin seeds – useful for those with nut allergies

Citrus

lime

lemon

orange

yuzu

Mushrooms

buna shimeji

chestnut

oyster

straw

button

eryngii

field

shiitake

enoki (enokitake)

Beans and other legumes

broad beans – buy frozen and use instead of edamame (soya) beans

edamame (soya) beans – keep a packet in the freezer

mangetout – cook in seconds when added to hot soups

sugarsnap peas

green beans

peas

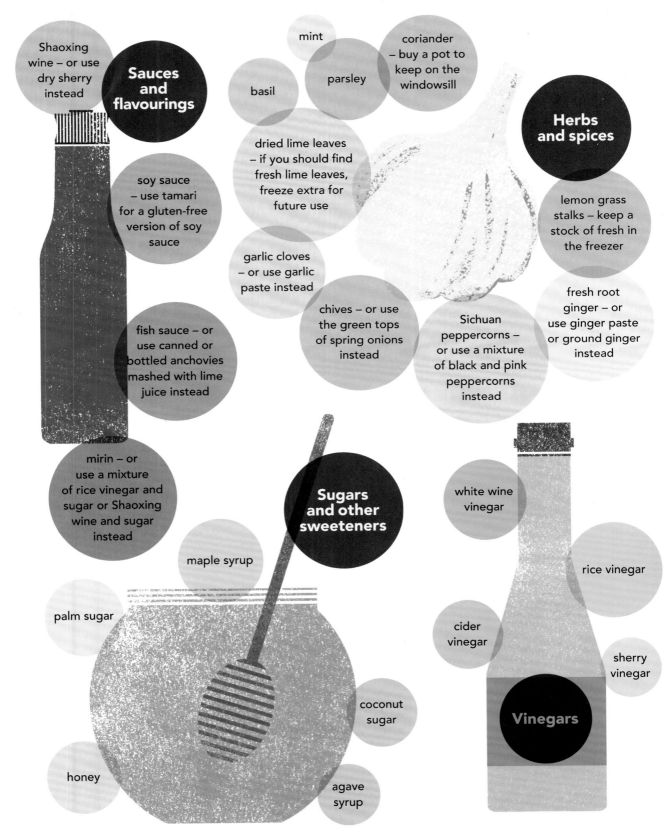

Shaoxing wine – or use dry sherry instead

Sauces and flavourings

mint

parsley

basil

coriander – buy a pot to keep on the windowsill

dried lime leaves – if you should find fresh lime leaves, freeze extra for future use

soy sauce – use tamari for a gluten-free version of soy sauce

garlic cloves – or use garlic paste instead

Herbs and spices

lemon grass stalks – keep a stock of fresh in the freezer

fish sauce – or use canned or bottled anchovies mashed with lime juice instead

chives – or use the green tops of spring onions instead

Sichuan peppercorns – or use a mixture of black and pink peppercorns instead

fresh root ginger – or use ginger paste or ground ginger instead

mirin – or use a mixture of rice vinegar and sugar or Shaoxing wine and sugar instead

Sugars and other sweeteners

white wine vinegar

maple syrup

rice vinegar

palm sugar

cider vinegar

sherry vinegar

coconut sugar

Vinegars

honey

agave syrup

Equipment

Ensuring that you have these items of kit in your kitchen will definitely make the preparation of your suppers even easier and quicker.

Saucepans with lids
If you have one large, medium and small-sized pan, you will be prepared for all eventualities. Well-fitting lids are invaluable when you want to heat things quickly or when you are cooking rice for locking in the moisture and steam.

Wok
This pan is essential for speedily stir-frying lots of ingredients together at once. It can reach a high temperature, which is vital for stir-frying, and its high sides mean you can toss and flip ingredients as you cook without them spilling out of the pan.

Steamer
The most versatile steamers are ones that fit over your saucepans (*see Time-saving Tips opposite*), either metal with a perforated base and a clear lid or a traditional bamboo steamer. Vegetables, fish and even meat can be cooked healthily, simply and quickly in this way.

Blender
This enables you to whizz up smooth soups and sauces effortlessly and in a flash. A stick blender is useful for blending small quantities of ingredients and also means you can blend a mixture directly in the cooking pan. However, a freestanding jug blender is ideal for blending larger amounts.

Big, sharp knife & large chopping board
Although it may look intimidating, a knife with a large blade will cut vegetables, fish and meat more efficiently, safely and quickly than one with a smaller blade. Make sure the blade is sharp – a roller-style knife sharpener will do the job easily and safely – and use it on a generously sized chopping board.

High-quality grater
Microplane make an excellent, razor-sharp grater that will turn garlic cloves and fresh root ginger into a paste with just a couple of strokes.

Measuring spoons
Recipes for sauces, where flavour balance is key, work much better if the ingredients are measured accurately.

Tongs
These are great for tossing noodles and salads or for turning hot food in frying pans and roasting trays.

Spiralizer &/or julienne peeler
You can make fantastic long fine strands of vegetable noodles using a spiralizer. If you don't have room in your kitchen for another gadget, use a julienne peeler, which looks like a potato peeler but has little teeth in the blade that cut elegant long thin strips.

Time-saving tips

- Fill saucepans with boiling water from the kettle instead of heating the water from cold.

- Cover saucepans with a well-fitting lid to keep the heat and moisture in and reduce cooking times.

- Steaming vegetables can be much quicker than boiling and helps retain the nutrients.

- Double up: when you are boiling noodles, put a steamer over the top of the saucepan and cook some vegetables at the same time.

- Never underestimate how useful a timer can be. It is essential for cooking rice, and allows you to get on with other jobs confident in the knowledge that you won't forget to take the pan off the heat when you need to.

- Use a large, sharp kitchen knife and a big chopping board to make preparation much quicker and easier, and you will be cutting up ingredients like a pro in next to no time!

- Fresh root ginger, garlic and chilli are often used and can be fiddly to peel or deseed and cut up. Buy them in paste form and add them by the teaspoon to reduce preparation time and effort.

- Alternatively, use a Microplane grater (*see opposite*) to shred garlic and fresh root ginger in moments.

- Fresh chilli adds a zingy heat to dishes, but chilli flakes make a great instant storecupboard substitute if you are in a real hurry.

Noodle & soup toppings

A sprinkle of these toppings over soups, salads, rice or noodles is an easy way to add extra texture and flavour. Keep some in your cupboard so that you can 'pimp up' a dish in an instant.

Toasted seeds, nuts & coconut

Sesame, sunflower and pumpkin seeds, cashew nuts and peanuts and flaked coconut are all great sprinkled over soups and salads – see, for example, the topping for the Sweet Potato, Tamarind & Coconut Soup on page 163. Alternatively, try toasting a handful of mixed nuts and seeds in a hot, dry frying pan over a medium–high heat for about 30 seconds until they start to smell toasted and the seeds begin to pop, then add 1 tablespoon of soy sauce and toss to coat.

Sheets of nori

You can buy these sheets of dried seaweed from large supermarkets or online. Just tear the sheets or cut up over salads, or slip half a sheet into ramen bowls, such as the Courgette Noodle Miso Ramen on page 31.

Ramen eggs

These are delicious added to ramen bowls, such as the Seafood Ramen on page 55 and the Courgette Noodle Miso Ramen on page 31, grain bowls or salads for some extra protein.

1. Cook fridge-cold free-range eggs in a saucepan of boiling water for 6 minutes.
2. Drain and shell the eggs while still warm.
3. Mix together equal quantities of soy sauce, mirin and sake, enough to cover the eggs, in a bowl – use a small one so that you need less liquid. Add the eggs and leave for 5–10 minutes to allow them to absorb the flavours of the sauce, then cut in half to serve.

noodles

Noodle cooking times

Noodles can vary greatly in size and cooking time, but here are some guidelines as to which method is best to use for what type of noodle and the time required. Also check the cooking instructions on the packet, and if you are ever unsure of cooking times, start testing for doneness a few minutes before the end of the specified time and that way you can make sure they are cooked until just tender.

Udon

These can be round or flat-shaped and are available dried or ready-cooked. They have a firm, chewy texture and, due to their thickness, they stay firm when added to broths or coated in sauces.

Cook dried udon for 6 minutes in plenty of boiling water – 1.5 litres (2¾ pints) for 100g (3½oz), enough for two servings, then add 500ml (18fl oz) per each additional 100g (3½oz). Ready-cooked udon can be added directly to hot broth to heat through or heated in the wok.

Egg noodles

These are often curly shaped, with a yellowish colour produced by the egg yolks used to make them. They have a firm texture with a good bite. Use them in stir-fries (their spirals are great for ensnaring other ingredients) as well as in ramen broths. These are the easiest noodles to eat with chopsticks!

Cook dried egg noodles by soaking them in a bowl of boiling water for 8 minutes, or cook in a saucepan of simmering water for 4 minutes.

Somen noodles

These straight noodles are delicate and skinny – only a little thicker than vermicelli – and are great eaten cold in salads where they retain some bite.

Cook for 5–6 minutes in plenty of boiling water.

Ramen noodles

These are similar to egg noodles but made without eggs. Their chewy texture instead comes from an alkaline solution mixed with the flour. They are often spiral shaped (but also come in a straight form) and are perfect for use in ramen bowls or other broths because they keep their bite after sitting in liquid. Look for wholewheat versions for a healthier alternative.

Cook instant ramen noodles by soaking in a bowl of boiling water for 3 minutes or in hot soup broth.

Gluten-free noodles

There are lots of noodle options to choose from if you want or need to avoid those made from wheat flour, which contain gluten.

Buckwheat (soba) noodles

When made with 100% buckwheat flour, these are gluten free, but check the label, as many varieties contain added wheat flour. Buckwheat noodles have a wonderful nutty flavour, but the texture can become soft, so they are best used in drier dishes such as stir-fries rather than soups or broths.

Cook for 6 minutes in plenty of boiling water, then drain and refresh under cold running water. This will help prevent them becoming too soft or sticking together.

Crystal noodles

Also called glass or cellophane noodles, these are made using vegetable starch (usually from mung beans) and are gluten free and often fat free. They live up to their name when cooked, producing transparent, crystal strands.

Cook for 3–6 minutes in plenty of boiling water, or as per packet instructions, just until they turn transparent and feel soft. Drain and refresh with plenty of cold water to remove any excess starch.

Rice noodles

These gluten-free noodles are made with white or brown rice and come dried in thick ribbons, thin ribbons and fine threads (vermicelli). With a silky texture and a chewy bite, they are delicious in soups, laksa (*see* page 44) and eaten cold in salads.

Cook by soaking in a bowl of boiling water for 4–8 minutes, depending on thickness. Drain and add directly to hot dishes or refresh under cold running water before adding to salads.

Other gluten-free noodles

Sweet potato (konjac), buckwheat and seaweed noodles (made from agar-agar) are also 100% gluten free and make great alternatives to wheat noodles for use in broths, stir-fries or salads.

Cook by soaking in boiling water until pliable – this will take 4–6 minutes, depending on thickness. Drain and add directly to hot dishes or refresh under cold running water before adding to salads.

Soba noodle salad with avocado & Asian pesto

Serves 4

➕ 626 calories

➖ 5.3g saturated fat

For the Asian pesto:

50g (1¾oz) bunch of coriander, plus
extra leaves to garnish

1 hot red chilli, seeds in, roughly
chopped

a thumb-sized piece of fresh root
ginger (about 20g/¾oz), peeled

1 garlic clove, peeled

1 tbsp mint leaves

1 tbsp toasted sesame oil

1 tbsp soy sauce

¼ tsp salt

1 tbsp lemon or lime juice

1 tbsp agave syrup

For the salad:

320g (11oz) dried buckwheat (soba)
noodles, 80g (2¾oz) per serving

2.5 litres (4½ pints) boiling water

1 tsp salt

1 tbsp toasted sesame oil

2 ripe avocados

4 tbsp sunflower seeds

4 tbsp pumpkin seeds

This glorious tangle of herb-coated noodles is teamed with creamy avocado and crunchy, toasted seeds. You can try out different sorts of noodles here – 100% buckwheat (soba) or sweet potato and buckwheat for a gluten-free dish, or skinny somen noodles for some extra bite.

To make the pesto:

1. Rinse the bunch of coriander under the tap, then shake it to remove most of the water. Roughly chop it, including the stalks, and put into a blender with the chilli.

2. Grate the ginger and garlic and add to the coriander in the blender, along with the remaining pesto ingredients.

3. Blend to a smooth sauce, then scrape into a large bowl and set aside.

To make the salad:

4. Cook the noodles in a large saucepan of the measured boiling water with the salt added for 6 minutes. Drain and refresh under cold running water, then toss with the sesame oil in a bowl.

5. Cut the avocados in half, remove the stone and peel, then cut the flesh into small cubes and add to the pesto in the large bowl.

6. Heat a dry frying pan, add the sunflower and pumpkin seeds and toast over a medium–high heat for about 30 seconds until they start to pop and smell toasted. Tip into a bowl to cool.

7. Add the noodles to the pesto and avocado and toss to mix. Divide between serving plates and sprinkle over the toasted seeds, then garnish with coriander leaves before serving.

Sweet potato, sesame & soba salad

Serves 2

⊕ 440 calories

♥ 2.4g saturated fat

60g (2¼oz) dried buckwheat (soba) noodles

1.5 litres (2¾ pints) boiling water

1 tsp salt

1 quantity Sesame Sauce (*see* page 189)

½ red cabbage, thinly sliced

2 sweet potatoes, peeled and cut into long thin strands or strips with a spiralizer or julienne peeler

handful of spinach, shredded

1 tbsp sesame seeds, preferably toasted

1 tsp chilli flakes

1 tbsp chopped chives

Dressed with itsu's favourite sesame sauce, this noodle salad is packed with healthy veg. Cooking the vegetables with the noodles means even faster preparation – and less washing-up!

1. Cook the noodles in a large saucepan of the measured boiling water with the salt added for 6 minutes.
2. While the noodles are cooking, make the sesame sauce (*see* page 189) and set aside.
3. A minute before the noodles are ready (after 5 minutes of cooking), add the cabbage, sweet potato strands or strips and spinach to the boiling water and cook together for the final minute.
4. Drain the noodles and vegetables and put into a large bowl with the sesame sauce.
5. Add the sesame seeds, chilli flakes and chives and toss well before serving.

Spiced udon & crunchy vegetables with crisp tofu

Serves 2

⊕ 465 calories

⊖ 2.8g saturated fat

100g (3½oz) dried udon noodles
  or 150g (5½oz) ready-cooked
  udon noodles
1.5 litres (2¾ pints) boiling water
½ tsp salt
½ white or red cabbage, sliced
1 yellow or red pepper, cored,
  deseeded and sliced
100g (3½oz) sugarsnap peas
1 quantity Spicy Udon Sauce
  (*see* page 188)
2 tbsp sesame seeds, preferably
  toasted, to serve

For the crisp tofu:
1 tbsp vegetable oil
150g (5½oz) firm tofu, cut into 1cm
  (½-inch) thick slices

This filling bowl of noodles has a lively kick of spice from the sauce. Full of colours and textures, it is a vegetarian option that provides all the ingredients you need for a balanced meal.

1. Cook the udon (if using dried) in a saucepan of the measured boiling water with the salt added for 6 minutes.
2. While the noodles are cooking, steam the cabbage and peppers for 4–6 minutes, adding the sugarsnap peas for the final 2 minutes of the cooking time. (If you are using ready-cooked udon, cook the vegetables for 3 minutes in the salted boiling water and add the udon for the final minute.)
3. Make the spicy udon sauce (*see* page 188) and set aside.
4. For the tofu, heat the oil in a nonstick frying pan until it is smoking. Pat the tofu slices dry with kitchen paper, add to the pan and fry over a high heat for about 30 seconds on each side until they are crisp and brown. Remove to a plate.
5. When cooked, drain the noodles (and vegetables if cooking together) well and put them into a large bowl. Add the steamed vegetables and crisp tofu and dress with the sauce.
6. Serve while hot, with the sesame seeds sprinkled over the top.

Time-saving tip: steam the vegetables over the saucepan you are cooking the noodles in so that they cook at the same time.

Udon with walnut miso & mushrooms

Serves 2

➕ 301 calories

❤ 1.7g saturated fat

1 quantity Walnut Miso Broth
    (*see* page 180)

100g (3½oz) dried udon noodles
    or 150g (5½oz) ready-cooked
    udon noodles

1.5 litres (2¾ pints) boiling water

1 tsp salt

300g (10½oz) Chinese or white
    cabbage, shredded

1 tbsp toasted sesame oil, to serve

4 spring onions, finely chopped,
    to serve

Walnuts and mushrooms are combined to give this simple broth a real depth of flavour. This is savoury comfort in a bowl.

1. Make the broth and leave to simmer, then prepare the walnut miso and set aside (*see* page 180).
2. Cook the udon (if using dried) in a large saucepan of the measured boiling water with the salt added for 6 minutes, adding the cabbage for the final minute of the cooking time. (If you are using ready-cooked udon, cook with the cabbage in the salted boiling water for 1 minute.) Drain the noodles and cabbage, then divide between 2 bowls.
3. Stir the walnut miso into the simmering broth.
4. Ladle the hot broth and mushrooms over the top of the noodles and cabbage, then sprinkle with the sesame oil and finely chopped spring onions before serving.

Broccoli, sweetcorn & egg noodles

Serves 2

➕ 562 calories

➖ 5.2g saturated fat

120g (4¼oz) dried egg noodles
2 tbsp groundnut oil
1 hot red chilli, chopped
2 garlic cloves, chopped
2 free-range eggs, beaten
1 head of broccoli, broken into
small florets
160g (5¾oz) canned sweetcorn
2 tbsp water
2 tbsp soy sauce
1 tbsp fish sauce
1 tbsp lime juice

This ultra-easy, quick stir-fry is packed with nutritious ingredients. Cooking vegetables in a really hot wok gives them a delicious toasted flavour.

1. Soak the noodles in a bowl of boiling water for 6 minutes, then drain.
2. Heat 1 tablespoon of the oil in a wok, add the chilli and fry over a high heat for a few seconds. Add the garlic and fry for about 30 seconds, then add the egg and cook, stirring, until it is no longer wet and is starting to colour.
3. Remove the cooked mixture from the wok, give the wok a quick wipe with kitchen paper and return to the heat.
4. Heat the remaining tablespoon of oil in the wok, add the broccoli and stir-fry over a high heat for 1 minute, allowing it to char slightly.
5. Add the sweetcorn, measured water and the soy and fish sauces. Stir well and cook for a couple of minutes until the broccoli is no longer raw but still has some bite.
6. Return the egg mixture to the wok and add the noodles, then toss everything together well and cook for 1 minute to heat through.
7. Sprinkle over the lime juice and toss again before serving.

Courgette noodle miso ramen

Serves 2

⊕ 403 calories

⊖ 3.8g saturated fat

1 quantity Ramen Chicken Miso Broth
   (*see* page 180)
1 head of spring greens, finely
   shredded
1 tsp salt
2 large courgettes, cut into long thin
   strands or strips with a spiralizer
   or julienne peeler
150g (5½oz) edamame (soya) beans
   or peas, frozen or fresh
black and white sesame seeds,
   preferably toasted, to garnish

For the toppings (optional):
1 sheet of nori, torn in half
2 Ramen Eggs (*see* page 13), halved

It is easy to create these courgette noodles using a spiralizer or a julienne peeler. Making ramen is a great excuse to include extra ingredients as toppings like seasonal vegetables, sheets of nori seaweed and soy-marinated eggs.

1. Make the broth, finely slicing the reserved white spring onion parts on the diagonal for the garnish (*see* page 180).
2. Cook the spring greens in a large saucepan of boiling water with the salt added for 1 minute. Scoop them out of the pan with a slotted spoon and refresh under cold running water.
3. Bring the water back to a rolling boil and cook the courgette noodles and beans or peas for 30 seconds or so, until they are no longer raw but still have some bite. Drain and refresh under cold running water.
4. When you are ready to serve, heat the broth to a simmer and add the cooked vegetables to warm through.
5. Divide the courgette noodles and broth between 2 bowls, then slip a half sheet of nori into the side of each bowl and top with the ramen eggs, if using. Sprinkle with the sliced spring onions and sesame seeds to garnish.

Time-saving tip: the cooked vegetables can be prepared in advance and kept covered in the fridge until needed.

Gluten-free chicken noodle salad

Serves 2

⊕ 136 calories

♡ 0.9g saturated fat

150g (5½oz) cooked chicken
    breast slices
1 head of pak choi, sliced
1 carrot, cut into long thin strands
    or strips with a spiralizer or
    julienne peeler
1 cucumber, cut into long thin
    strands or strips with a spiralizer
    or julienne peeler
1 shallot, thinly sliced
40g (1½oz) mixed coriander and
    basil with a few mint leaves,
    roughly chopped
40g (1½oz) roasted salted peanuts,
    roughly chopped
1 quantity Thai Salad Dressing
    (see page 186)

This speedy, summery salad is created using colourful raw vegetable noodles, crunchy peanuts and a zingy Thai dressing.

1. Mix all the salad ingredients except the dressing together in a large bowl.
2. Make the Thai salad dressing (see page 186), then pour over the salad and toss well before serving.

Vermicelli & vegetable miso

Serves 2

➕ 370 calories

➖ 0.4g saturated fat

100g (3½oz) dried vermicelli
    rice noodles

800ml (1⅓ pints) ready-made
    vegetable stock (*see* page 180)

2 tbsp miso paste

2 tbsp soy sauce

20g (¾oz) ginger paste

100g (3½oz) green beans, topped
    and cut into short lengths, or
    sugarsnap peas

2 carrots, cut into 5mm (¼-inch) coins

1 head of fennel, trimmed and
    thinly sliced

100g (3½oz) tenderstem broccoli,
    roughly chopped

100g (3½oz) bean sprouts

2 spring onions, chopped

Fine rice noodles give this healthy miso broth some extra body, for a light yet satisfying supper.

1. Soak the noodles in a bowl of boiling water for 4 minutes, then drain and refresh under cold running water.
2. While the noodles are soaking, bring the stock to the boil in a saucepan and stir in the miso, soy sauce and ginger paste.
3. Add the green beans and carrots to the stock and boil for 2 minutes.
4. Add the fennel and broccoli and cook for 2–3 minutes more, then turn off the heat and stir in the bean sprouts.
5. Pile the noodles into 2 bowls and ladle the soup over. Sprinkle with the spring onions and serve.

Vietnamese vegetable pho

Serves 2

- 317 calories
- 0.3g saturated fat

1 quantity Vietnamese Vegetable Broth
   (*see* variation on page 181)
100g (3½oz) dried thick rice noodles
100g (3½oz) chestnut or shiitake
   mushrooms, sliced
2 carrots, cut into long thin strands
   or strips with a spiralizer or
   julienne peeler
2 heads of pak choi (about 200g/7oz),
   stalks and leaves separated and
   sliced
50g (1¾oz) bean sprouts
1 hot red chilli, thinly sliced
40g (1½oz) mixed coriander and basil
   with a few mint leaves, roughly torn
1 lime, halved

A vegetarian version of the classic Vietnamese noodle soup, this is a supper bowl packed with health and flavour – the itsu way.

1. Make the Vietnamese vegetable broth (*see* page 181) leaving it to simmer while you prepare the other ingredients.
2. Soak the noodles in a bowl of boiling water for 8 minutes, then drain and refresh under cold running water.
3. After the broth has simmered for 10 minutes, strain into a jug, discarding the solids, and return to the saucepan.
4. Bring the broth back to the boil and add the mushrooms, carrot strands or strips and pak choi stalks. Cook for a couple of minutes before adding the pak choi leaves.
5. Divide the noodles between 2 bowls, ladle the broth and vegetables into each bowl and scatter the bean sprouts, chilli and torn herbs over the top. Serve with half a lime each, to squeeze over.

Egg noodles & shiitake with green onion & sesame sauce

Serves 2

⊕ 592 calories

♥ 4.6g saturated fat

150g (5½oz) dried egg noodles
1 quantity Green Onion & Sesame
    Sauce (*see* page 185)
1 tbsp groundnut oil
200g (7oz) shiitake or chestnut
    mushrooms, sliced
40g (1½oz) fresh root ginger, peeled
    and thinly sliced
300g (10½oz) baby leaf spinach

To serve:

20g (¾oz) bunch of coriander,
    roughly chopped
2 tablespoons black and white sesame
    seeds, preferably toasted

Stir-fried gingery mushrooms and spinach are tossed with a punchy sauce and a tangle of noodles.

1. Soak the noodles in a bowl of boiling water for 8 minutes, then drain and refresh under cold running water.
2. While the noodles are soaking, make the Green Onion & Sesame Sauce (*see* page 185).
3. Heat the oil in a wok and stir-fry the mushrooms and ginger over a high heat for 3–4 minutes until the mushrooms are coloured all over.
4. Add the spinach and stir-fry until just wilted. Then add the sauce and the noodles and toss well until heated through.
5. Sprinkle with the chopped coriander and the sesame seeds to serve.

Vegetarian Singapore noodles

Serves 2

⊕ 558 calories

⊖ 5.5g saturated fat

100g (3½oz) dried vermicelli
    rice noodles
2 tbsp groundnut oil
1 hot green chilli, finely chopped
1 tsp ginger paste
1 tsp garlic paste
2 spring onions, chopped
3 free-range eggs
100g (3½oz) green beans, topped
150g (5½oz) peas, frozen or fresh
2 carrots, julienned or sliced
10g (¼oz) coriander, roughly chopped

For the sauce:
½ tsp curry powder
2 tbsp soy sauce
2 tbsp Shaoxing wine or dry sherry
1 tbsp fish sauce

In this Singapore-style noodle stir-fry, the egg soaks up all the flavours of the sauce and provides the requisite protein to supplement the vegetables.

1. Soak the noodles in a bowl of boiling water for 3 minutes, then drain and refresh under cold running water.
2. Mix all the sauce ingredients together in a small bowl and set aside.
3. Prepare all the other ingredients and place them next to the hob so that they are close at hand when you start to stir-fry.
4. Heat the oil in a wok, add the chilli and fry over a high heat for a few seconds. Then add the ginger and garlic pastes and spring onions and fry for about 30 seconds.
5. Crack the eggs into the wok and stir to break up the yolks. Fry until the egg forms small, cooked particles.
6. Add the green beans, peas and carrots and all the sauce ingredients. Toss to coat, then cook for 3–5 minutes until the beans are no longer raw but still have some bite.
7. Add the noodles to the wok along with the coriander and toss everything together well just long enough to heat the noodles through and so that they become well coated in the sauce.

Variation: if you are craving a 'meatier' alternative, cooked chicken, pork or prawns can always be added.

Pad spiralizer

Serves 2

⊕ 623 calories

⊖ 8g saturated fat

1 tbsp groundnut oil

1 shallot, chopped

2 garlic cloves, thinly sliced

2 free-range eggs, beaten

200g (7oz) cooked peeled prawns

2 large courgettes, cut into long thin strands or strips with a spiralizer or julienne peeler

2 handfuls of bean sprouts

8 radishes, roughly chopped

2 tbsp chopped chives

100g (3½oz) roasted salted peanuts, roughly chopped by hand or in a food processor

For the sauce:

2 tbsp lime juice

1 hot red chilli, deseeded and chopped

1 tbsp soy sauce

1 tbsp fish sauce

1 tsp agave syrup, maple syrup or palm sugar

An 'inspiralized' take on the classic rice noodle dish pad Thai, this recipe uses courgette noodles to create a juicier and even healthier alternative. But it can be made with rice noodles too.

1. Mix all the sauce ingredients together in a bowl until well combined, then set aside.
2. Prepare all the other ingredients and place them next to the hob so that they are close at hand when you start to stir-fry.
3. Heat the oil in a wok until very hot, then add the shallot and stir-fry over a high heat for 1 minute before adding the garlic.
4. When the garlic is starting to colour, add the beaten eggs, stirring all the time so that it scrambles. Before it is completely cooked, add the prawns.
5. Toss and stir the egg and prawns until the egg is cooked through, then add the courgette noodles and the prepared sauce.
6. Give the ingredients a good toss and leave to cook and steam for a couple of minutes so that the courgette is no longer raw.
7. Add the remaining ingredients and mix well before piling onto 2 plates to serve.

Squash & coconut laksa

Serves 4

- 382 calories
- 6.9g saturated fat

1 tbsp groundnut oil
1 tsp garlic paste
2 tsp ginger paste
1 tsp chilli flakes
½ lemon grass stalk, finely chopped
4 dried lime leaves
500g (1lb 2oz) ready-prepared
   diced butternut squash and/
   or sweet potato, or peeled and
   deseeded butternut squash and/
   or sweet potato, cut into 1cm
   (½-inch) chunks
1 red onion, cut into wedges
1 tbsp fish sauce
½ tsp salt
500ml (18fl oz) ready-made chicken
   stock (*see* page 180)
400ml (14fl oz) can coconut milk
200g (7oz) dried wide rice noodles or
   2 x 150g (5½oz) packets ready-
   cooked rice noodles
½ lime
20g (¾oz) bunch of coriander,
   roughly chopped, to serve

The rice noodles take on a silky texture in this sweet, coconut sauce – in fact, the word 'laksa' derives from an ancient Persian word for noodles, *lakhsha*, meaning slippery. For super-speedy preparation, use ready-chopped vegetables.

1. Heat the oil in a saucepan. Add the garlic and ginger pastes, chilli flakes, lemon grass and lime leaves and cook over a medium heat, stirring, for 1 minute before adding the squash and/or sweet potato, onion, fish sauce and salt.
2. Add the stock and coconut milk and increase the heat to high. Cover with a lid, bring to the boil and cook for 8–10 minutes, or until the squash and/or sweet potato is soft to the point of a knife.
3. Meanwhile, soak the noodles (if using dried) in boiling water for 8 minutes, then drain and refresh under cold running water.
4. When the squash and/or sweet potato is cooked, add the soaked or ready-cooked noodles, squeeze the lime half over and stir well until warmed through. Serve with the coriander scattered over each bowl.

Variation: instead of the butternut squash and/or sweet potato, use green vegetables such as broccoli, mangetout or Chinese cabbage for an alternative flavour – and they will cook even faster!

Udon, salmon & spicy leaves

Serves 2

✚ 625 calories

◗ 3.4g saturated fat

170g (6oz) dried udon noodles

1.5 litres (2¾ pints) boiling water

1 tsp salt

2 tbsp miso paste

2 tbsp soy sauce

150g (5½oz) salmon fillet, skinned
    and cut into small pieces

150g (5½oz) mixed watercress and
    rocket leaves, roughly chopped

100g (3½oz) bean sprouts

2 spring onions, thinly sliced

1 tbsp sesame seeds, preferably
    toasted

1 tbsp toasted sesame oil

The watercress and rocket wilted into the miso broth add a peppery bite, providing a great foil for the omega-3 oil-rich salmon.

1. Cook the udon in the measured boiling water in a large saucepan for 6 minutes with the salt, then drain and refresh under cold running water.
2. While the noodles are cooking, put the miso in a cup or small bowl and mix in 2 tablespoons boiling water to soften it slightly and make a smooth liquid paste.
3. Pour another 500ml (18fl oz) boiling water into a large saucepan and add the miso along with the soy sauce.
4. Bring the liquid to the boil and add the salmon pieces. Simmer for 1 minute until just cooked through, then scoop out the salmon and set aside.
5. Add the chopped watercress and rocket to the hot liquid, stirring so that the leaves wilt.
6. After about 1 minute, add the bean sprouts and the salmon, then turn off the heat.
7. Divide the noodles between 2 bowls, pour the hot broth over the noodles and spoon over the wilted leaves, salmon and bean sprouts.
8. Sprinkle with the spring onions, sesame seeds and sesame oil before serving.

Vietnamese seafood pho

Serves 2

⊕ 342 calories

♥ 0.4g saturated fat

1 quantity Vietnamese Fish Broth
    (*see* page 181)
40g (1½oz) dried thin rice noodles
100g (3½oz) mushrooms – try to find
    enoki (enokitake), otherwise use
    chestnut or button mushrooms,
    sliced
handful of spinach or any spring greens
    (*see* page 9), finely shredded
150g (5½oz) uncooked seafood per
    person, a mixture of any of the
    following: peeled prawns; squid,
    cut into strips; scallops, halved;
    clams in their shells; 1cm (½-inch)
    pieces of firm white fish fillet, such
    as monkfish, hake or sea bass
1 hot red chilli, deseeded and diced
2 spring onions, finely chopped
2 handfuls of bean sprouts (optional)
1 lime, halved

This is perfect summer sustenance – warming yet deliciously refreshing. If you should come across fresh lime leaves for making the broth, they can be kept in the freezer and used from frozen when needed, as with lemon grass stalks.

1. Make the fish broth, reserving the coriander leaves for later, leaving it to simmer while you prepare the other ingredients (*see* page 181).
2. Soak the noodles in a bowl of boiling water for 5 minutes, then drain and refresh under cold running water.
3. After the broth has simmered for 10 minutes, strain into a jug, discarding the solids, and return to the saucepan.
4. Bring the broth back to the boil, add the mushrooms and spinach or other greens and cook for 2 minutes.
5. Add the seafood and cook for a further 2–3 minutes until just cooked through.
6. Divide the noodles and pho between 2 bowls, sprinkle over the chilli, spring onions, bean sprouts, if using, and reserved coriander leaves, and squeeze the lime over before serving.

Prawn & ginger noodle salad

Serves 4

⊕ 269 calories

⊖ 1.5g saturated fat

100g (3½oz) dried vermicelli rice
    noodles
1 cucumber, cut into long thin
    strands or strips with a spiralizer
    or julienne peeler
150g (5½oz) cherry tomatoes, halved
250g (9oz) cooked peeled prawns
4 spring onions, chopped
60g (2¼oz) roasted salted peanuts,
    roughly chopped
40g (1½oz) mixed coriander and basil
    with a few mint leaves, roughly
    chopped
1 quantity Thai Salad Dressing
    (*see* page 186)

A super-flavourful salad that takes very little time to prepare, this tastes great in a lunch box or to eat the following day.

1. Soak the rice noodles in a bowl of boiling water for 4 minutes, then drain and refresh them under cold running water.
2. While the noodles are soaking, prepare the salad ingredients, put into a large bowl and mix well.
3. Make the Thai salad dressing (*see* page 186), then add to the salad along with the noodles. Toss well before serving.

Smoked mackerel soba

Serves 2

➕ 406 calories

🖤 3.4g saturated fat

100g (3½oz) dried buckwheat
    (soba) noodles

1.5 litres (2¾ pints) boiling water

3 tbsp miso paste

2 tbsp soy sauce

1 head of pak choi, sliced

100g (3½oz) smoked mackerel,
    skinned and flaked

2 spring onions, chopped

2 tbsp sesame seeds, preferably
    toasted

¼ tsp black pepper

Mackerel is packed with health-giving omega oils, and its smokiness imparts a wonderful depth of flavour to this simple miso broth.

1. Cook the noodles in the measured boiling water in a large saucepan for 6 minutes, then drain and refresh under cold running water.
2. While the noodles are cooking, bring 800ml (1⅓ pints) water to the boil in a separate saucepan. Put the miso in a cup or small bowl and mix with the soy sauce to soften it slightly and make a smooth liquid paste, then whisk into the pan of water to combine.
3. Reduce the miso broth to a simmer, add the pak choi and mackerel flakes and cook for 2–3 minutes.
4. Divide the noodles between 2 bowls, pour the hot broth over the noodles and spoon the pak choi and mackerel equally into each bowl.
5. Sprinkle with the spring onions, sesame seeds and black pepper before serving.

Seafood ramen

Serves 4

- 350 calories
- 2.2g saturated fat

200g (7oz) dried wheat noodles
  (use dried egg noodles or instant
  ramen noodles – *see* pages 16–17)
1 quantity Seafood Ramen Broth
  (*see* page 180)
500g (1lb 2oz) seafood, such as
  uncooked or cooked peeled
  prawns; squid, cut into strips;
  scallops, halved; cooked white
  crabmeat

To serve:

4 spring onions, chopped
2 Ramen Eggs (*see* page 13), halved
  (optional)
4 sheets of nori (optional)

Try to find the freshest seafood available, and use one or two types or a mixture of them all. Top with nori and ramen eggs for a sophisticated supper in minutes.

1. Cook the noodles as described on pages 16–17, then drain and refresh under cold running water.
2. While the noodles are cooking, make the seafood ramen broth (*see* page 180).
3. Add the seafood to the broth and simmer for 2–3 minutes, or until the larger pieces of seafood are just cooked.
4. Divide the noodles between 4 bowls and ladle the broth and seafood equally over each.
5. Sprinkle with the spring onions, and add a ramen egg half and a sheet of nori tucked into the side of each bowl, if using, to serve.

Chilli prawn & chicken stir-fry

Serves 2

➕ 427 calories

♥ 3g saturated fat

100g (3½oz) dried udon noodles
  or 150g (5½oz) ready-cooked
  udon noodles
1.5 litres (2¾ pints) boiling water
2 tbsp groundnut oil
1 garlic clove, sliced
4 spring onions, sliced
2 hot green chillies, chopped
175g (6oz) cooked peeled prawns
150g (5½oz) boneless, skinless
  chicken, sliced into small pieces
200g (7oz) ripe tomatoes, chopped
1 red pepper, cored, deseeded
  and chopped
juice of ½ lime
2 tbsp soy sauce
1 tbsp fish sauce
10g (¼oz) coriander, roughly
  chopped

The texture of thick udon noodles works best with this dish – you can use wok-ready ones for added convenience and speed. Prawns and chicken are a classic Asian combination, and both provide a good source of protein with relatively little fat.

1. Cook the udon (if using dried) in a saucepan of the measured boiling water for 6 minutes, then drain and refresh under cold running water.
2. While the noodles are cooking, prepare all the other ingredients and place them next to the hob so that they are close at hand when you start to stir-fry.
3. Heat 1 tablespoon of the oil in a wok, add the garlic, spring onions and chillies and fry over a high heat for 30 seconds until they start to colour.
4. Add the prawns and chicken and stir-fry for a couple of minutes. When the chicken starts to brown and feel firm, remove everything to a plate.
5. Heat the remaining tablespoon of oil in the wok, add the tomatoes and red pepper and stir-fry for a few minutes so that the tomatoes start to become juicy and the pepper softens. Then add the lime juice and soy and fish sauces and return the chicken and prawns to the pan.
6. Toss everything together well, then add the cooked or ready-cooked noodles and toss again until they are warmed through.
7. Sprinkle with the chopped coriander and toss once more before serving.

Chicken & vegetable stir-fry

Serves 2

➕ 430 calories

❤ 0.8g saturated fat

100g (3½oz) dried egg noodles

1 tbsp soy sauce

1 tbsp oyster sauce

juice of ½ lime

4 tbsp groundnut or vegetable oil

250g (9oz) boneless, skinless chicken breast, sliced into small pieces

100g (3½oz) sweet potato, peeled and cut into thin, wide ribbons with a vegetable peeler

1 large courgette, cut into fine sticks

1 hot red chilli, deseeded and finely chopped

1 tsp garlic paste

1 tsp ginger paste

1 bunch of spring greens or other greens (*see* page 9), cut into thin shreds

3 spring onions, finely chopped

20g (¾oz) bunch of coriander, roughly chopped

The beauty of stir-fried dishes is that they take only minutes to cook and can be packed with flavour and nourishing vegetables, so they are super healthy too.

1. Soak the noodles in a bowl of boiling water for 6 minutes, then drain and refresh under cold running water.
2. While the noodles are soaking, mix the soy and oyster sauces and lime juice together in a bowl and set aside.
3. Prepare all the other ingredients and place them next to the hob so that they are close at hand when you start to stir-fry.
4. Heat 2 tablespoons of the oil in a wok until very hot. Add the chicken, which should sizzle and smoke immediately, so if not, increase the heat. Cook over a high heat, stirring and moving the pieces around in the wok so that they don't stick, for a minute or so until they are nicely browned. Remove to a plate.
5. Heat the remaining 2 tablespoons of oil in the wok, add the sweet potato and stir-fry over a high heat for 1 minute until it softens and starts to colour.
6. Add the courgette to the wok and stir-fry for 30 seconds or so, then throw in the chilli with the garlic and ginger pastes and stir briskly.
7. Next add the greens and spring onions to the wok and cook, tossing and stirring, for another minute until the greens begin to wilt.
8. Finally, drop the noodles into the wok, pour the soy sauce mixture over the top and toss briefly to reheat the noodles and coat everything with the sauce.
9. Scatter with the coriander and serve on warmed plates.

Chicken miso ramen

Serves 2

⊕ 673 calories

⊖ 6.4g saturated fat

2 chicken breasts, skin on, about
 200–250g (7–9oz) each
1 quantity Ramen Chicken Miso Broth
 (*see* page 180)
100g (3½oz) dried wheat noodles
 (use dried egg noodles or instant
 ramen noodles – *see* pages 16–17)

For the chicken marinade:
1 tbsp miso paste
1 tbsp soy sauce
2 tsp groundnut oil

For the ramen vegetables:
½ head of spring greens, finely
 shredded
1 courgette, sliced
100g (3½oz) peas or edamame (soya)
 beans, frozen or fresh

For the toppings:
2 spring onions, chopped
1 sheet of nori, torn in half (optional)
2 Ramen Eggs (*see* page 13), halved
 (optional)

This simple-to-prepare ramen is ultimate comfort food in a bowl. Adding miso to chicken stock gives it an extra, umami-packed dimension. Be sure to use chicken breasts with the skin on for maximum flavour.

1. Preheat the oven to 220°C (425°F), Gas Mark 7.
2. Mix the marinade ingredients together in a bowl. Rub into the chicken breasts on a roasting tray.
3. Roast the chicken breasts for 12 minutes, or until cooked through, turning once halfway through.
4. While the chicken is roasting, make the ramen chicken miso broth (*see* page 180).
5. Cook the noodles as described on pages 16–17, then drain.
6. Return the strained broth to the saucepan and bring to the boil. Add the ramen vegetables and cook for 3–4 minutes until just tender.
7. Slice the cooked chicken breasts, reserving any roasting juices to pour over the dish.
8. Divide the noodles between 2 bowls, ladle over the ramen broth and vegetables, adding the reserved chicken roasting juices, and lay the pieces of chicken over the top.
9. Sprinkle with the spring onions, and add a half sheet of nori and a ramen egg half, if using, to each bowl before serving.

itsu classic chicken noodles

Serves 2

⊕ 505 calories

♥ 8g saturated fat

100g (3½oz) dried vermicelli
　　noodles or 150g (5½oz)
　　ready-cooked noodles
1 leek, trimmed, cleaned and
　　thinly sliced
150g (5½oz) frozen edamame (soya)
　　beans, or peas or broad beans
150g (5½oz) cooked chicken
　　breast slices
20g (¾oz) bunch of coriander,
　　roughly chopped

For the broth:

800ml (1⅓ pints) ready-made
　　chicken stock (*see page 180*)
25g (1oz) creamed coconut
1 tsp ginger paste
½ tsp garlic paste
1 tbsp soy sauce
1 tsp agave syrup
½ tsp ground coriander
½ tsp ground turmeric
½ tsp ground cumin
1 hot green chilli, finely chopped
½ lemon grass stalk, finely chopped
1 tbsp lime juice

Juicy chicken and noodles are dished up in a deliciously flavoured broth. Simply adding a few storecupboard ingredients to chicken stock takes it to a whole new level.

1. To make the broth, put the chicken stock with all the other broth ingredients into a large saucepan and bring to the boil.
2. Meanwhile, soak the noodles (if using dried) in a bowl of boiling water for 4 minutes, then drain and refresh under cold running water.
3. Add the leek to the broth and boil for 3 minutes, then add the beans, or peas, and cook for a further 2 minutes.
4. Finally, add the chicken and coriander to the broth with the soaked or ready-cooked noodles and heat through for 1 minute before serving.

Hoisin duck noodles

Serves 2

- 659 calories
- 4.6g saturated fat

2 duck breasts, about 200g (7oz) each
2 tsp Chinese five-spice powder
1 tsp groundnut oil
140g (5oz) dried egg noodles
1 tbsp toasted sesame oil
3 tbsp hoisin sauce
3 tbsp soy sauce
2 tbsp rice vinegar or lime juice
1 cucumber, cut into long thin
    strands or strips with a spiralizer
    or julienne peeler
2 spring onions, chopped, to serve

The rich flavour of duck is delicious dressed with Chinese five-spice powder and hoisin sauce, while the cucumber adds a fresh flavour and crunchy texture.

1. Preheat the oven to 220°C (425°F), Gas Mark 7.
2. Score the skin of the duck breasts in a criss-cross pattern with a sharp knife. Rub the five-spice powder and groundnut oil into the duck skin and meat.
3. Place the duck on a roasting tray and roast for 15 minutes.
4. Meanwhile, soak the noodles in a bowl of boiling water for 8 minutes, then drain and toss with the sesame oil in a bowl.
5. Mix the hoisin sauce, soy sauce and rice vinegar or lime juice with the cucumber in another bowl, then add this to the noodles.
6. Slice the cooked duck breast and add to the noodles, then sprinkle over the chopped spring onions to serve.

Noodles in chicken broth

Serves 2

➕ 250 calories

🔽 0.2g saturated fat

100g (3½oz) dried egg noodles

800ml (1⅓ pints) ready-made chicken stock (*see* page 180)

a thumb-sized piece of fresh root ginger (about 20g/¾oz), peeled and cut into fine sticks

2 hot red or green chillies, deseeded and chopped

4 spring onions, chopped

2 tbsp oyster sauce

2 tbsp soy sauce

This bowl of pure comfort takes less than 15 minutes to prepare – the ultimate healthy storecupboard supper!

1. Soak the noodles in a bowl of boiling water for 8 minutes, then drain.
2. While the noodles are soaking, put the chicken stock in a large saucepan with all the other ingredients and bring to the boil.
3. When the noodles are cooked, add them to the broth and leave for 1 minute to absorb the flavours.
4. Scoop the noodles into 2 bowls (a pair of tongs is a useful tool for this) and ladle the broth over the top to serve.

itsu chicken Jaipur

Serves 2

➕ 677 calories

🖤 13.1g saturated fat

100g (3½oz) dried vermicelli
    rice noodles or 200g (7oz)
    ready-cooked noodles
1 leek, trimmed, cleaned and
    thinly sliced
1½ tbsp raisins
150g (5½oz) frozen edamame
    (soya) beans
150g (5½oz) cooked chicken
    breast slices
20g (¾oz) bunch of coriander,
    roughly chopped

For the jaipur broth:

800ml (1⅓ pints) ready-made
    chicken stock (*see* page 180)
1 tbsp tomato purée
1 tsp agave syrup
½ tsp ground coriander
½ tsp ground cumin
½ tsp ground turmeric
1 tsp garlic paste
1 tsp ginger paste
¼ tsp salt
3 tbsp crème fraîche

A mix of fragrant storecupboard spices and flavourings added to ready-made chicken stock makes this delicious itsu classic effortless to recreate at home.

1. To make the broth, put the chicken stock in a large saucepan with all the other broth ingredients and bring to the boil.
2. Meanwhile, soak the noodles (if using dried) in boiling water for 4 minutes, then drain and refresh under cold running water.
3. Add the leek and raisins to the chicken broth and boil for 3 minutes, then add the beans and cook for a further 2 minutes.
4. Finally, add the chicken and coriander to the broth with the soaked or ready-cooked noodles and heat through for 1 minute before serving.

Minced chilli pork noodles

Serves 4

➕ 801 calories

🔻 6g saturated fat

400g (14oz) dried egg noodles
 (or other noodles of your choice –
 see pages 16–17)
2 tbsp groundnut oil
4 spring onions, chopped
2 garlic cloves, sliced
2 hot red chillies, chopped
500g (1lb 2oz) organic or free-range
 minced pork
20g (¾oz) bunch of coriander and
 a few sprigs of mint, roughly
 chopped, to serve

For the sauce:
2 tbsp oyster sauce
2 tbsp soy sauce
1 tbsp fish sauce
1 tbsp agave syrup or palm sugar

Try different types of noodles to go with this spicy pork mince – any buckwheat variety would work well instead of egg noodles. It is worth choosing organic or free-range minced pork, as it has a better flavour and texture when cooked.

1. Soak the noodles in a bowl of boiling water for 8 minutes, then drain and set aside.
2. While the noodles are soaking, mix all the sauce ingredients together in a bowl and set aside.
3. Prepare all the other ingredients and place them next to the hob so that they are close at hand when you start to stir-fry.
4. Heat the oil in a wok, add the spring onions, garlic and chillies and stir-fry over a high heat for a few seconds until they start to colour.
5. Add the minced pork and fry over a high heat for a few minutes, breaking up any lumps, until it starts to colour. If it releases any water, continue frying until it evaporates and the pork starts to colour.
6. Add the sauce and the noodles to the wok and cook for a further minute or so, tossing to combine, until the noodles have heated through.
7. Sprinkle with the chopped herbs to serve.

Pork & mushrooms with cucumber noodles

Serves 2

⊕ 391 calories

♥ 3.2g saturated fat

2 tbsp groundnut or vegetable oil

1 hot red chilli, very finely chopped

2 garlic cloves, chopped

150g (5½oz) mushrooms (*see* page 10), sliced

¼ tsp salt, plus extra if needed

200g (7oz) pork fillet, sliced into 5mm (¼-inch) strips

1 large cucumber, cut into long thin strands or strips with a spiralizer or julienne peeler

For the sauce:

1 tbsp rice vinegar

1 tbsp lime juice, plus extra to serve if needed

1 tbsp fish sauce

2 tsp agave syrup

Spiralized or long julienned strands or strips of cucumber make a great (and skinnier) alternative to wheat or rice noodles. The deep flavours of the pork and mushrooms are given a zingy burst of flavour with this fresh-tasting sauce.

1. Mix all the sauce ingredients together in a bowl and set aside.
2. Prepare all the other ingredients and place them next to the hob so that they are close at hand when you start to stir-fry.
3. Heat 1 tablespoon of the oil in a wok and fry the chilli over a high heat for a few seconds.
4. Add the garlic, mushrooms and half the salt and stir-fry for a couple of minutes until any liquid released by the mushrooms has evaporated and they have shrunk and softened. Remove to a plate.
5. Wipe the wok with a piece of kitchen paper, then add the remaining tablespoon of oil and heat until smoking hot.
6. Add the pork strips and the remaining salt and stir-fry over a high heat just until the meat changes from raw pink to brown and cooked.
7. Return the mushrooms to the wok, add the cucumber strands or strips and the sauce and toss well. Cook just long enough to heat the cucumber. Taste for salt and add more lime juice if necessary before serving.

Beef shabu-shabu with udon

Serves 2

- 452 calories
- 3.4g saturated fat

100g (3½oz) dried udon noodles
1.5 litres (2¾ pints) boiling water
½ tsp salt
100g (3½oz) shiitake or chestnut
    mushrooms, sliced
1 leek, trimmed, cleaned and sliced
½ white or Chinese cabbage, shredded
2 spring onions, chopped
2 tbsp soy sauce
2 tbsp lime or lemon juice
2 tbsp mirin
2 tsp rice vinegar
1 tsp sesame paste or tahini
200g (7oz) beef fillet, very thinly sliced

This is an adaptation of a classic Japanese dish where slices of extra-lean and tender beef cook in hot broth. The key is to slice the beef really thinly so that it cooks quickly.

1. Cook the udon in a large saucepan of the measured boiling water with the salt for 6 minutes, then drain and refresh under cold running water.
2. While the noodles are cooking, pour 800ml (1⅓ pints) boiling water into a separate large saucepan and add the mushrooms and leek. Bring back to the boil, cover with a lid and cook for 2–3 minutes.
3. Add the cabbage and cook, covered, for 2 minutes.
4. Add the spring onions, soy sauce, lime or lemon juice, mirin, rice vinegar and sesame paste or tahini and stir well as it comes to the boil, then add the noodles to heat through.
5. Divide the noodles between 2 bowls and lay the beef slices over the top. Ladle the boiling broth and vegetables over the beef and noodles, stirring to submerge and cook the beef in the hot broth before serving.

Beef pho

Serves 2

✚ 424 calories

⊘ 2.3g saturated fat

1 quantity Vietnamese Beef Broth
   (*see* page 181)
120g (4¼oz) dried wide rice noodles
150g (5½oz) beef fillet, thinly sliced
2 handfuls of bean sprouts
½ red onion, very thinly sliced
2 limes, halved

Infusing the stock with aromatic spices gives this noodle dish its distinctive Vietnamese flavour. The slices of ultra-lean beef fillet cook very quickly, which means you can still create this deeply flavourful and satisfying meal when you have no time to spare.

1. Make the Vietnamese beef broth, reserving the coriander leaves for serving, leaving it to simmer while you prepare the other ingredients (*see* page 181).
2. Soak the rice noodles in boiling water for 6 minutes, then drain and refresh under cold running water.
3. After the broth has simmered for 10 minutes, strain into a jug, discarding the solids, and return to the saucepan.
4. Bring the broth back to the boil, add the beef slices and cook for 1 minute, or until the meat turns from red to pink.
5. Divide the noodles, beef and broth between 2 bowls and top with the bean sprouts and red onion. Tear the reserved coriander leaves and scatter over. Squeeze a lime half over each serving and serve with the other half to add more as needed.

Chilli peanut beef noodles

Serves 2

- 434 calories
- 3.7g saturated fat

100g (3½oz) dried buckwheat (soba) noodles
1.5 litres (2¾ pints) boiling water
10 Sichuan peppercorns or a mixture of black and pink peppercorns
20g (¾oz) roasted salted peanuts, roughly chopped
2 tbsp groundnut or vegetable oil
100g (3½oz) curly kale, tough stalks removed, torn into small pieces
140g (5oz) lean minced beef
1 whole dried red chilli, deseeded and chopped, or 1 tsp chilli flakes
a thumb-sized piece of fresh root ginger (about 20g/¾oz), peeled and chopped
1 garlic clove, chopped
1 tbsp toasted sesame oil

For the sauce:
1 tbsp Shaoxing wine or dry sherry
1 tbsp soy sauce
1 tsp rice vinegar

Full of nutty flavours from the peanuts and buckwheat noodles, this dish also has an added kick from the chilli.

1. Cook the noodles in a large saucepan of the measured boiling water for 6 minutes, then drain and refresh under cold running water.
2. While the noodles are cooking, prepare all the other ingredients and place them next to the hob so that they are close at hand when you start to stir-fry.
3. Heat a dry wok, add the peppercorns and peanuts and toast over a medium–high heat until they start to colour. Remove to a plate.
4. Heat 1 tablespoon of the groundnut or vegetable oil in the wok, add the kale and stir-fry over a high heat for a couple of minutes so that it starts to smell toasted and begins to wilt but still has some bite. Remove to a plate.
5. Heat the remaining tablespoon of groundnut or vegetable oil in the wok, add the minced beef and fry over a high heat for a few minutes, breaking up any lumps, until it starts to colour. If it releases any water, continue frying until it evaporates and the beef starts to colour.
6. Add the dried chilli or chilli flakes, ginger and garlic and stir-fry for a further minute.
7. Return the peppercorns and peanuts to the wok with the kale, add the sauce ingredients and toss together well, then cook for 1 minute.
8. Finally, add the noodles with the sesame oil and cook, tossing to combine, for a few moments to heat through before serving.

Summer beef noodle salad

Serves 4

✚ 241 calories

♥ 2.4g saturated fat

50g (1¾oz) dried vermicelli rice
    noodles
200g (7oz) beef fillet, thinly sliced
150g (5½oz) green beans, topped,
    or sugarsnap peas
1 quantity Thai Salad Dressing
    (*see* page 186)
2 carrots, julienned
½ Chinese or white cabbage, shredded
1 small red onion, thinly sliced
40g (1½oz) roasted salted peanuts,
    roughly chopped
50g (1¾oz) mixed coriander and basil
    with a few mint leaves, roughly
    chopped

This fresh-tasting, enlivening salad is perfect for warm, sunny days. It makes great leftovers too!

1. Soak the noodles in a bowl of boiling water for 4 minutes, then drain and refresh under cold running water.
2. Put the beef slices in a bowl and pour over boiling water to cover. Leave for 2 minutes, then drain.
3. Blanch the green beans or sugarsnap peas in a saucepan of boiling water for 2 minutes, then drain and set aside.
4. Make the Thai salad dressing (*see* page 186).
5. Put all the remaining salad ingredients into a bowl with the cooked noodles. Add the dressing and toss everything well before serving.

Variation: you can use leftover roast beef instead of uncooked beef fillet, cut into small strips.

rice & grains

Types of rice

Brown rice

Brown rice still has its husks in place, so it has a nuttier flavour and a chewier texture and contains more fibre and nutrients than white rice, which has had the outside husk removed. However, it does take longer to cook, so look for **ready-cooked brown rice** or **ready-cooked brown rice and grains** mixtures. Try it with the Cauliflower, Coconut & Pea Curry on page 122.

Long-grain white rice

Basmati rice and **jasmine rice** are well-known, widely available varieties of long-grain white rice. They are less starchy than short-grain varieties and cook to produce a firmer-textured rice, with grains that stay separate rather than sticking together.

Wild rice

Like brown rice, wild rice grains also still have their husks in place, so have a similar nutty flavour and chewy texture and contain more fibre and nutrients than white rice. To avoid long cooking times, look for **uncooked white basmati and wild rice mixtures** that cook in under 20 minutes (check the label to avoid choosing those with longer cooking times, or use a ready-cooked mixture instead). These taste great served with the Hoisin Roast Duck Breast on page 105.

Short-grain white rice

There are a number of varieties that you will already know – **Italian risotto rice**, **Spanish paella rice** and **Japanese-style short-grain (sushi) rice** as well as **pudding rice**. If you can't find Japanese-style short-grain rice, choose another short-grain white variety – it can be prepared using the same simple method to produce a delicious, sticky textured rice in under 20 minutes (see page 88).

Types of grain

❶ Gluten-free grains

Quinoa, amaranth, buckwheat and millet are all gluten-free whole grains that can be cooked in under 20 minutes. You can also try mixing several of these whole grains together to create a dish of varied textures.

Quinoa (**1**, top left) is a great alternative to rice and is packed with protein and vitamins. **Amaranth** (**1**, top right) can be cooked quickly to produce tiny, caviar-like popping grains, which are great in salads or dressed with a sauce and served as a side dish with meat or fish. **Buckwheat** (**1**, bottom left) has larger grains than quinoa and amaranth and a firmer, nuttier texture. **Millet** (**1**, bottom right) produces plump, yellow grains rather like a large, sticky form of couscous.

❷ Wheat grain products

Couscous (**2**, bottom right), **pearl barley** (**2**, top right), **faro** (**2**, bottom left) and **bulgar wheat** (**2**, top left), which all contain gluten as they are derived from wheat, can be served hot as an alternative to rice or other grains, providing a different flavour and texture. With added herbs and fresh vegetables, they can also be used to make delicious salads – *see* the Quinoa, Salmon & Vegetable Bowl on page 125 or Teriyaki Chicken Potsu on page 90. There is now a great selection of these grains available ready-cooked from mini supermarkets for extra convenience.

❸ Meat-free protein for rice & grains

Canned or **ready-cooked lentils** (**3**, top right) and **chickpeas** (**3**, bottom right) and **frozen edamame (soya) beans** or **broad beans** (**3**, bottom left), all of which are legumes, can be used to add protein as well as great bite and taste to rice and grain dishes, especially ones that don't contain meat. See, for example, Rice & Lentils (Kitchari) on page 130.

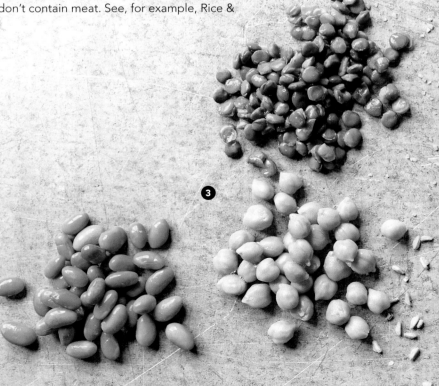

Cooking rice & grains

Japanese-style sticky rice

Serves 2

➕ 269 calories

💙 trace saturated fat

150g (5½oz) uncooked Japanese-style
   short-grain white rice
200ml (7fl oz) water
pinch of salt

1. Put the rice into a small saucepan
   with the measured water and salt
   and bring to the boil.
2. Cover with a lid, reduce the heat a
   little and cook for 10 minutes.
3. Turn off the heat and leave to stand,
   covered, for 8 minutes to allow the
   rice to steam.

Boiled basmati or other long-grain white rice

Serves 4

➕ 272 calories

💙 0.1g saturated fat

300g (10½oz) uncooked basmati or
   other long-grain white rice
¼ tsp salt

1. Put the rice into a saucepan and
   cover with water by 2cm (¾ inch).
   Add the salt and bring to the boil.
2. Cover with a lid, reduce the heat a
   little and cook for 5 minutes.
3. Turn off the heat and leave to stand
   and steam, covered, for 5 minutes.

Steamed basmati or other long-grain white rice

Serves 2

➕ 272 calories

💙 0.1g saturated fat

150g (5½oz) uncooked basmati or
   other long-grain white rice
150ml (¼ pint) water
¼ tsp salt

1. Choose a saucepan with a lid and
   a heatproof bowl that will fit inside
   the pan, with a space at least 4cm
   (1½ inches) wide around the outside
   of the bowl.
2. Pour boiling water into the saucepan.
3. Put the rice, measured water and
   salt into the heatproof bowl and
   place in the saucepan. Cover with
   the lid and boil for 15 minutes.
4. Turn off the heat, then remove the
   lid and fluff up the rice with a fork.
   Re-cover the rice and leave to steam
   until needed.

Quinoa

Serves 2

⊕ 154 calories

♥ 0.3g saturated fat

100g (3½oz) uncooked quinoa
200ml (7fl oz) water
½ tsp salt

1. Put the quinoa in a saucepan with the measured water and salt and bring to the boil.
2. Reduce the heat to low, cover with a lid and cook for 10–12 minutes until just tender.

Amaranth

Serves 2

⊕ 185 calories

♥ 0.7g saturated fat

100g (3½oz) uncooked amaranth
200ml (7fl oz) water
¼ tsp salt

1. Put the amaranth in a saucepan with the measured water and salt and bring to the boil.
2. Reduce the heat to low, cover with a lid and cook for 12 minutes.
3. Turn off the heat and leave to stand, covered, for 3 minutes to allow the amaranth to steam.

Millet

Serves 2

⊕ 177 calories

♥ 0.2g saturated fat

100g (3½oz) uncooked millet
150ml (¼ pint) water
¼ tsp salt

1. Put the millet in a saucepan with the measured water and salt and bring to the boil.
2. Reduce the heat to low, cover with a lid and cook for 12 minutes.

Buckwheat

Serves 2

⊕ 170 calories

♥ 0.3g saturated fat

100g (3½oz) uncooked buckwheat
200ml (7fl oz) water
¼ tsp salt

1. Put the buckwheat in a saucepan with the measured water and salt and bring to the boil.
2. Reduce the heat to low, cover with a lid and cook for 15 minutes.

Teriyaki chicken potsu

Serves 2

⊕ 333 calories

♥ 1.9g saturated fat

For the chicken:

2 boneless, skinless chicken breasts,
about 200–250g (7–9oz) each

1 tbsp teriyaki sauce

1 tbsp groundnut oil

For the vegetables:

1 red pepper, cored, deseeded
and sliced

1 carrot, sliced

100g (3½oz) mushrooms (*see* page 10),
sliced

100g (3½oz) mangetout

1 head of pak choi, sliced

To finish:

1 quantity Ginger Teriyaki Sauce
(*see* page 187)

250g (9oz) ready-cooked brown rice,
or spelt or another grain

**Potsu is itsu's unique idea of a layered bowl of goodness
– healthy rice or grains, protein, vegetables and a
delicious sauce. It offers the ideal opportunity to choose
whatever grain you like for the base from the great
variety now available ready-cooked including brown rice,
spelt and quinoa.**

For the chicken:

1. Preheat the oven to 220°C (425°F), Gas Mark 7.
2. Put the chicken breasts on a roasting tray and sprinkle with
    the teriyaki sauce and oil, turning them over a couple of
    times to coat well. Roast for 12 minutes, or until cooked
    through, turning once halfway through.
3. Once cooked, remove from the oven and leave until cool
    enough to handle, then slice into strips.

For the vegetables:

4. While the chicken is roasting, steam the red pepper, carrot
    and mushrooms together for 3 minutes.
5. Add the mangetout and pak choi and steam for a further
    2–3 minutes until all the vegetables are just tender but still
    with a little crunch.

To finish:

6. Make the ginger teriyaki sauce (*see* page 187).
7. Put the rice or grain into a small saucepan with about a
    tablespoon of water over a high heat, cover and warm
    through for 2 minutes, stirring at intervals.
8. Serve the rice or grain with the vegetables piled on top,
    covered with the chicken slices and the sauce poured over.

Red coconut curry potsu

Serves 2

➕ 594 calories

➖ 13.5g saturated fat

1 quantity Red Coconut Curry Sauce
(*see* page 189)

2 boneless, skinless chicken breasts,
about 200–250g (7–9oz) each, cut
into bite-sized pieces

2 tsp groundnut oil

250g (9oz) ready-cooked white rice or
brown rice, or quinoa

100g (3½oz) curly kale, tough stalks
removed, torn into small pieces

1 spring onion, finely chopped,
to serve

salt and black pepper

Another of itsu's special layered meals in a bowl, this one features chicken and curly kale laid on a bed of rice or quinoa, covered in a spicy, coconut sauce.

1. Preheat the oven to 220°C (425°F), Gas Mark 7.
2. Meanwhile, make the Red Coconut Curry Sauce
(*see* page 189).
3. Toss the chicken pieces in the oil on a roasting tray, then
season with salt and pepper and a tablespoon of the
red coconut curry sauce. Roast for 8–10 minutes, or until
cooked thoroughly, turning once halfway through.
4. While the chicken is roasting, put the rice or quinoa into
a small saucepan with about a tablespoon of water over a
high heat, cover and warm through for 2 minutes, stirring
at intervals.
5. Steam the kale for 3 minutes until tender.
6. Divide the rice or quinoa between 2 bowls, lay the kale
and chicken pieces over the top and cover with the
remaining Red Coconut Curry Sauce. Sprinkle with the
finely chopped spring onion before serving.

Miso-rubbed chicken on sticky rice

Serves 2

⊕ 493 calories

⊖ 5.1g saturated fat

100g (3½oz) uncooked Japanese-style
    short-grain white rice
180ml (6fl oz) water
4 boneless chicken thighs, skin on
1 tbsp miso paste
1 tbsp soy sauce
2 tbsp groundnut oil
200g (7oz) sugarsnap peas
4 spring onions, chopped
2 tsp rice vinegar
salt and black pepper

These miso-coated roasted chicken pieces are satisfyingly sticky, with crunchy sugarsnaps and starchy glutinous rice complementing them perfectly.

1. Preheat the oven to 220°C (425°F), Gas Mark 7.
2. Cook the rice with a pinch of salt and the measured water as described on page 88.
3. While the rice is cooking, make 4 deep cuts in each chicken thigh with a sharp knife. Mix the miso, soy sauce and 1 tablespoon of the oil together in a bowl to make a paste and rub it into the chicken so that it is well coated.
4. Place the chicken thighs in a baking dish and roast for 10–15 minutes until the skin is crisp and the meat is cooked through – test by inserting a knife; the juices that run out should be clear.
5. Meanwhile, boil or steam the sugarsnaps for 3 minutes, then drain, if necessary, and toss with the remaining tablespoon of oil and a large pinch of salt and black pepper to taste.
6. When the rice is cooked, add the spring onions and rice vinegar and stir through.
7. Serve the miso chicken with the rice and sugarsnaps, with any roasting juices poured over.

Chicken & eggs on rice

Serves 2

➕ 382 calories

➖ 2.1g saturated fat

300ml (½ pint) ready-made chicken
    stock (*see* page 180)

2 tbsp soy sauce

1 tsp agave syrup

200g (7oz) boneless, skinless chicken
    breasts, sliced into finger-wide
    pieces, or cooked chicken breasts,
    torn into strips

3 spring onions, sliced

2 free-range eggs, stirred to break up
    the yolk but not beaten

250g (9oz) ready-cooked Japanese-
    style short-grain white rice

For the toppings (optional):

1 tbsp black sesame seeds,
    preferably toasted

shredded strips of nori

Although sticky rice has been used here, basmati or other long-grain white rice would also work well. This dish is best made with fresh liquid chicken stock rather than using a stock cube. Serve with wilted greens for a splash of colour.

1. Put the stock into a saucepan with the soy sauce and agave syrup and bring to the boil.
2. Add the chicken and spring onions to the stock and reduce the heat to a simmer. Cook for 1–2 minutes, or until the chicken is no longer pink (if using uncooked chicken).
3. Pour in the eggs and increase the heat, stirring gently as the eggs form colourful white and yellow strands while they cook in the stock. When the stock starts to bubble up around the sides of the pan, remove the pan from the heat.
4. Meanwhile, put the rice into a small saucepan with about a tablespoon of water over a high heat, cover and warm through for 2 minutes, stirring at intervals.
5. Divide the rice between 2 bowls. Ladle the chicken and egg along with lots of stock over each bowl, then top with the sesame seeds and strips of nori, if using.

Chicken katsu

Serves 4

⊕ 479 calories

⊖ 2.4g saturated fat

1 tbsp vegetable oil

2 large carrots, cut into
    semicircular discs

1 large onion, chopped

½ tsp salt

1 tbsp ginger paste

1 tsp garlic paste

1 tbsp tomato purée

1 tsp chilli powder

1 tsp Chinese five-spice powder

1 tsp ground turmeric

350g (12oz) boneless, skinless chicken
    thighs, cut into 1cm (½-inch) pieces

200ml (7fl oz) ready-made chicken
    stock (*see* page 180)

1 tbsp cornflour or potato flour

1 tbsp water

200ml (7fl oz) milk or soya milk

20g (¾oz) bunch of coriander,
    roughly chopped, to serve

For the quinoa rice

100g (3½oz) uncooked quinoa

100g (3½oz) uncooked basmati rice

400ml (14fl oz) water

½ tsp salt

Katsu is Japan's answer to curry sauce. To make prepping this dish even easier and quicker, you can buy ready-cooked mixed quinoa and rice, or chickpeas and spelt for a change.

1. For the quinoa rice, put the quinoa and basmati into a saucepan with the measured water and salt and mix together. Cover with a lid and bring to the boil, then reduce the heat a little and cook for 12 minutes.

2. Meanwhile, heat the oil in a heavy-based flameproof casserole with a lid or saucepan and add the carrots, onion and salt. Cover with the lid and cook over a medium heat for a couple of minutes so that the vegetables soften.

3. Add the ginger and garlic pastes, tomato purée, spices and chicken and stir well. Let the mixture fry together for a further minute or so before adding the chicken stock.

4. Put the cornflour or potato flour into a cup or small bowl and mix with the measured water to a smooth paste, then stir into the katsu along with the milk.

5. Bring to a simmer, stirring well, then re-cover and cook for 10 minutes, stirring occasionally.

6. To serve, spoon the quinoa rice into bowls, top with the katsu and sprinkle over the coriander.

Chicken & quinoa salad with peanut sauce

Serves 2

⊕ 602 calories

◑ 8.2g saturated fat

4 tbsp Peanut Sauce (*see* page 185)
250g (9oz) ready-cooked quinoa
¼ red onion, very thinly sliced
1 cucumber, cut into small pieces
    or into long thin strands with
    a spiralizer
250g (9oz) cooked chicken slices
10g (¼oz) coriander leaves with
    1 tbsp mint leaves, roughly torn,
    to garnish

For the dressing:
1 tbsp olive oil
juice of 1½ limes
½ tsp salt

Quinoa offers nutritious protein and vitamins to make this a filling, energy-giving salad. The peanut sauce tastes especially good with slices of juicy chicken.

1. Make the peanut sauce (*see* page 185).
2. Put the quinoa, red onion, cucumber and chicken into a large bowl and gently mix together.
3. Stir in the peanut sauce, then add all the dressing ingredients and mix well.
4. Garnish with the torn coriander and mint leaves.

Chicken & chestnut donburi

Serves 4

⊕ 429 calories

♥ 3.2g saturated fat

200g (7oz) uncooked Japanese-style
  short-grain white rice
250ml (9fl oz) water
¼ tsp salt, plus an extra pinch of salt
  for the cooking water
2 tbsp sunflower or groundnut oil
250g (9oz) boneless, skinless chicken
  thighs, cut into small pieces
15g (½oz) fresh root ginger, peeled
  and finely chopped
1 garlic clove, finely chopped
3 tbsp soy sauce
1 tbsp mirin
2 small white onions, cut into quarters
1 leek, trimmed, cleaned and cut into
  thin rings
70g (2½oz) shiitake or chestnut
  mushrooms, quartered
100g (3½oz) ready-cooked chestnuts
250ml (9fl oz) ready-made chicken
  stock (*see* page 180)

**This is a great one-pot casserole dish, full of rich,
autumnal flavours.**

1. Cook the rice with the measured water and pinch of salt
   as described on page 88.
2. While the rice is cooking, heat 1 tablespoon of the oil in a
   heavy-based flameproof casserole with a lid or saucepan,
   add the chicken pieces and fry over a high heat for
   1 minute until they start to colour. Remove to a plate.
3. Add the remaining tablespoon of oil to the pan and fry
   the ginger and garlic over a medium–high heat for a few
   seconds until they start to colour.
4. Pour in the soy sauce and mirin and let the mixture begin
   to boil, then return the chicken to the pan and stir to coat
   well in the sauce.
5. Add the onions, leek, mushrooms and chestnuts, chicken
   stock and ¼ teaspoon of salt. Bring to the boil, then cover
   with the lid and cook over a medium heat for 7 minutes.
6. Serve the chicken and vegetables on a bed of the rice,
   with plenty of sauce spooned over the top.

Hoisin roast duck breast

Serves 2

- ⊕ 508 calories
- ⊖ 3.2g saturated fat

100g (3½oz) uncooked white basmati
    rice or 250g (9oz) ready-cooked
    wild rice and basmati
2 duck breasts, about 200g (7oz) each
1 tsp vegetable oil, plus 1 tbsp
1 quantity Stir-fry Sauce (*see* page 185)
200g (7oz) sugarsnap peas, or green
    beans, topped
salt

Hoisin and duck are made for each other, and this is a sauce that you will keep coming back to. You can use a mixture of wild rice and basmati here for a variation in texture and a nuttier flavour than white rice alone.

1. Preheat the oven to 220°C (425°F), Gas Mark 7.
2. Cook the rice (if using uncooked) with ¼ teaspoon of salt as described on page 88.
3. While the rice is cooking, score the skin of the duck breasts in a criss-cross pattern with a sharp knife. Rub all over with ½ teaspoon of salt and the teaspoon of oil.
4. Heat the tablespoon of oil in an ovenproof frying pan and fry the duck breasts, skin-side down, for 1 minute until they start to colour. Turn them over and transfer the pan to the oven to roast for 12 minutes.
5. While the duck is roasting, make the stir-fry sauce (*see* page 185).
6. When the duck is cooked but still pink inside, remove from the pan to a board. Pour the sauce mixture into the hot frying pan (remember not to touch the handle without oven gloves!) and heat until it starts to bubble.
7. Cut the duck breasts into slices and return to the pan to coat in the sauce.
8. Meanwhile, steam the sugarsnaps or beans for 3 minutes. (If using ready-cooked wild rice, put into a small saucepan with about a tablespoon of water over a high heat, cover and warm through for 2 minutes, stirring at intervals.)
9. Serve the rice with the duck slices and sugarsnaps or beans on top, with the sauce poured over it.

Miso salmon & rice with peas & ginger sauce

Serves 2

➕ 796 calories

♥ 5.6g saturated fat

100g (3½oz) uncooked Japanese-style short-grain white rice

300ml (½ pint) water

¼ tsp salt

150g (5½oz) frozen edamame (soya) beans or peas, or a mixture of both

400g (14oz) piece of salmon fillet, skin on, cut into 2 pieces

1 tbsp groundnut or vegetable oil

soy sauce, to serve

For the glaze:

2 tbsp mirin

1 tbsp sake or dry white wine

1½ tbsp miso paste

1 tsp agave syrup

For the ginger sauce:

40g (1½oz) fresh root ginger, peeled and roughly chopped

1 quantity Green Onion & Sesame Sauce (*see* page 184)

The miso glaze caramelizes as the fish cooks under the grill, giving it extra sweetness and flavour. Served with sticky rice, brightened by the peas and ginger sauce, it makes a sophisticated yet quick and easy dinner.

1. Heat the grill to a medium–high heat.
2. Cook the rice with the measured water and salt as described on page 88 also adding the beans or/and peas to the pan.
3. While the rice is cooking, put all the glaze ingredients into a small saucepan and heat, stirring, to a smooth liquid, then pour over the salmon fillets on a plate, turning them to coat completely.
4. Heat an ovenproof frying pan over a high heat, add the oil and heat until smoking hot. Place the salmon fillets in the pan, skin-side down, and brush with the remaining glaze from the plate. Fry for 1 minute, then place the frying pan under the grill and cook for 8–10 minutes, depending on the thickness of the fillets. The surface should appear browned and glazed when it is ready and the flesh just cooked through.
5. Meanwhile, put all the sauce ingredients into a jug and use a stick blender to blend to a sauce.
6. To serve, remove the salmon from the frying pan by sliding a metal spatula between the flesh and the skin, leaving the skin in the pan. Put a salmon fillet on each plate. Spoon a mound of the rice and beans or/and peas next to it and serve with the ginger sauce and soy sauce.

Egg fried rice & prawns

Serves 2

⊕ 646 calories

⊗ 6.1g saturated fat

4 free-range eggs, beaten

4 spring onions, chopped, white and
    green parts kept separate

3 tbsp light olive or other vegetable oil

2 carrots, finely chopped

1 tsp sea salt

200g (7oz) cooked peeled prawns

350g (12oz) ready-cooked long-grain
    white rice

One of the best uses for ready-cooked rice is to make this speedy, tasty supper. It is ultra simple, yet bursting with flavour.

1. Mix the eggs with the white parts of the spring onions.
2. Heat 2 tablespoons of the oil in a large frying pan or wok over a medium–high heat, add the eggs and allow them to form a layer over the base of the pan, as if you are making an omelette. When the egg has started to fry and set, gently stir it with a spoon, breaking it up into large pieces. When the pieces are cooked through and starting to brown, remove to a plate.
3. Add the remaining tablespoon of oil to the pan and fry the carrots with ½ teaspoon of the salt over a medium–high heat for a couple of minutes until it becomes soft and sweet.
4. Add the green parts of the spring onions and the prawns and fry over a high heat for a couple of minutes until they colour and smell aromatic.
5. Add the rice and the remaining ½ teaspoon of salt, stir well to coat all the grains and let them start to fry.
6. Return the egg to the rice and stir both together well before serving.

Steamed sea bass with green quinoa

Serves 2

➕ 403 calories

❤ 1.6g saturated fat

2 sea bass fillets, about 200g (7oz) each
1 lemon grass stalk, roughly chopped
10g (¼oz) fresh root ginger, peeled
   and sliced
1 hot red chilli, chopped
4 lime slices

For the green quinoa:
100g (3½oz) uncooked quinoa
150ml (¼ pint) water
½ tsp salt
1 quantity Asian Pesto (*see* page 187)

Steaming is one of the easiest ways to cook fish and keep it juicy. This is a great-looking dish, vibrant green in colour and brimming with healthy herbs.

1. Preheat the oven to 200°C (400°F), Gas Mark 6.
2. To make the green quinoa, cook the quinoa with the measured water and salt as described on page 89.
3. While the quinoa is cooking, place each sea bass fillet on a sheet of foil and scatter the remaining ingredients equally between them. Wrap up the foil into parcels, place on a baking sheet and bake for 10–12 minutes, depending on the thickness of the fish.
4. Meanwhile, make the pesto (*see* page 187).
5. When the quinoa is cooked, stir the pesto into it.
6. Serve the fish, unwrapped, with the juices from the parcel poured over it, next to a mound of green quinoa.

Miso-glazed cod & sesame rice

Serves 2

➕ 594 calories

➖ 1.8g saturated fat

2 cod loin fillets, about 200g (7oz) each
1 tbsp vegetable or light oil, such as
    groundnut or sunflower
2 heads of pak choi, sliced
100g (3½oz) sugarsnap peas
2 tbsp soy sauce

For the sesame rice:
150g (5½oz) uncooked Japanese-style
    short-grain white rice
200ml (7fl oz) water
¼ tsp salt
2 tbsp sesame seeds, preferably
    toasted

For the glaze:
2 tbsp mirin
1 tbsp sake or dry white wine
1½ tbsp miso paste
1 tsp agave syrup

This sweet-sticky miso glaze takes plain cod fillets to another level. Accompanied by a pile of sesame-flavoured glutinous rice, it makes the perfect supper.

1. Heat the grill to medium–high.
2. Cook the rice with the measured water and salt as described on page 88.
3. While the rice is cooking, put all the glaze ingredients into a small saucepan and heat, stirring, to a smooth liquid, then pour over the cod fillets on a plate, turning them to coat completely.
4. Heat an ovenproof frying pan over a high heat, add the oil and heat until smoking hot. Place the cod fillets in the pan, skin-side down, and brush with the remaining glaze from the plate. Fry for 30 seconds, then place the frying pan under the grill and cook for 8–10 minutes, depending on the thickness of the fillets. The surface should appear browned and glazed when it is ready and a skewer pushed into the fish should meet no resistance.
5. While the cod is cooking, cook the pak choi and sugarsnaps in a saucepan of boiling water for 2 minutes, then drain and season with the soy sauce.
6. When the rice is cooked, stir in the sesame seeds.
7. To serve, place a cod fillet on each plate, scraping up any caramelized juices from the pan to pour over, and spoon a mound of the rice and the greens next to it.

Teriyaki salmon & ginger rice

Serves 2

- 663 calories
- 5.6g saturated fat

100g (3½oz) uncooked Japanese-style
   short-grain white rice
180ml (6fl oz) water
pinch of salt
15g (½oz) peeled and grated fresh
   root ginger
2 salmon fillets, about 200g (7oz) each
2 tbsp teriyaki sauce
1 tsp salt
2 heads of pak choi
1 tbsp toasted sesame oil
1 tbsp vegetable oil
2 tbsp water
1 tbsp black sesame seeds,
   preferably toasted

**Teriyaki salmon is an all-time favourite at itsu and here
is a simple version for making at home. The ginger rice
provides the ideal accompaniment to the sweet sauce.**

1. Preheat the oven to 220°C (425°F), Gas Mark 7.
2. Cook the rice with the measured 180ml (6fl oz) water and
   salt as described on page 88, also adding 10g (¼oz) of the
   grated ginger to the pan.
3. While the rice is cooking, place the salmon fillets on a
   plate and pour over the teriyaki sauce, the remaining
   ginger and ½ teaspoon of the salt. Turn the fillets over
   several times to coat them completely.
4. Cut the pak choi into quarters or sixths lengthways
   (depending on their thickness) and lay on a roasting tray
   or in a baking dish. Sprinkle with the remaining ½ teaspoon
   of salt and the sesame oil. Place in the oven.
5. Heat an ovenproof frying pan over a high heat, add the
   vegetable oil and heat until smoking hot. Place the salmon
   fillets, skin-side down, in the pan. (Keep the plate with
   any remaining teriyaki marinade on it for later.) Fry for
   1 minute, then transfer the pan to the oven, above the pak
   choi, for 8 minutes, or until the fish is just cooked through.
6. Remove the fish from the pan and put the reserved
   teriyaki marinade along with the measured 2 tablespoons
   of water into the frying pan, then heat until bubbling to
   create a sauce.
7. Place each fish fillet on a plate with the rice and pak choi.
   Pour the sauce over and sprinkle with black sesame seeds
   before serving.

Smoked mackerel teriyaki & egg fried rice

Serves 2

➕ 554 calories

➖ 8.9g saturated fat

100g (3½oz) cooked long-grain white rice

2 free-range eggs, lightly beaten

¼ tsp salt

150g (5½oz) smoked mackerel, skinned

a thumb-sized piece of fresh root ginger (about 20g/¾oz), peeled and grated

4 tbsp teriyaki sauce

3 tbsp groundnut oil

4 spring onions, chopped

100g (3½oz) spring greens or other firm-leafed greens, shredded

black pepper

This super-speedy, protein-rich supper is based on cooked rice – you can either use a pack of ready-cooked rice or any leftover cooked rice you may have.

1. Put the cooked rice in a bowl with the eggs, the salt and black pepper to taste. Mix well to separate the rice and coat every grain.
2. Flake the mackerel into a separate bowl and add the ginger and teriyaki sauce.
3. Heat 2 tablespoons of the oil in a wok, add the rice and stir-fry over a medium–high heat for 1 minute until the egg starts to colour and dry out. Remove from the wok to a bowl and set aside.
4. Heat the remaining tablespoon of oil in the wok, add the spring onions and stir-fry over a high heat for a few seconds. Then add the greens and stir-fry for 1 minute until they start to wilt.
5. Add the mackerel and continue cooking just long enough for it to heat through.
6. Return the rice to the wok and toss everything together well before piling onto plates to serve.

Prawns, peanut sauce & sesame rice

Serves 4

➕ 379 calories

🔻 5.8g saturated fat

200g (7oz) uncooked Japanese-style
    short-grain white rice
250ml (9fl oz) water
¼ tsp salt
1 quantity Peanut Sauce (*see* page 185)
2 tbsp vegetable oil
4 spring onions, chopped
300g (10½oz) cooked peeled prawns
200g (7oz) tenderstem broccoli
1 tbsp black sesame seeds,
    preferably toasted

To serve:
chopped coriander
lime wedges

This wonderful nutty sauce can be used on all sorts of other ingredients too. Try it with grilled chicken skewers, or as a dressing for steamed or fried vegetables.

1. Cook the rice with the measured water and salt as described on page 88.
2. While the rice is cooking, make the peanut sauce (*see* page 185).
3. Heat 1 tablespoon of the oil in a wok until smoking hot, then add the spring onions and stir-fry over a high heat for a few seconds until they start to colour and soften.
4. Add the prawns and stir-fry for a further 30 seconds until they begin to brown. Remove the spring onions and prawns to a plate.
5. Heat the remaining tablespoon of oil in the wok, add the tenderstem broccoli and stir-fry briefly over a high heat before returning the prawns to the wok.
6. Pour the peanut sauce over and give it all a good toss, adding a few tablespoons of hot water from the kettle to create a coating sauce. Cover the wok with a lid and cook for a minute or so until the broccoli softens a little but still has a crunch.
7. When the rice is cooked, stir in the sesame seeds.
8. Arrange a pile of rice on each plate and pile the satay-coated prawns and broccoli on top. Sprinkle with chopped coriander and serve with lime wedges.

Stir-fried mixed seafood with sesame & ginger rice

Serves 2

➕ 469 calories

➖ 1.8g saturated fat

2 tbsp vegetable oil

1 shallot or small white onion,
    thinly sliced

1 garlic clove, sliced

1 hot green chilli, chopped

5g (⅛oz) fresh root ginger, peeled
    and sliced

150g (5½oz) uncooked or cooked
    peeled prawns

100g (3½oz) squid rings

4 scallops, halved

2 tsp tamarind paste

1 tbsp fish sauce

1 tbsp soy sauce

1 lime, quartered, plus extra to serve

chopped coriander, to serve

For the sesame & ginger rice:

100g (3½oz) uncooked Japanese-
    style short-grain white rice

180ml (6fl oz) water

pinch of salt

1 tsp peeled and grated fresh
    root ginger

1 spring onion, finely chopped

1 tbsp soy sauce

1 tbsp black sesame seeds,
    preferably toasted

You can choose any mixed seafood, often sold frozen in packs (remember to leave in the fridge to defrost before using) – mussels, prawns, scallops, squid or even small pieces of firm white fish work well.

1. For the sesame & ginger rice, cook the rice with the measured water and salt as described on page 88.
2. While the rice is cooking, prepare all the other ingredients and place them next to the hob so that they are close at hand when you start to stir-fry.
3. Heat 1 tablespoon of the oil in the wok until smoking hot, add the shallot or onion, garlic, chilli and ginger and stir-fry over a high heat for about 30 seconds until the shallot or onion colours and starts to soften. Tip everything out onto a plate and set aside.
4. Heat the remaining tablespoon of oil in the wok, and when it is really hot, add the seafood and stir-fry over a high heat for a couple of minutes until cooked through and starting to colour.
5. Return the shallot/onion mixture to the wok and add the tamarind and fish and soy sauces. Squeeze over the juice from 2 lime quarters and turn off the heat.
6. When the rice is ready, stir into it the grated ginger, spring onion, soy sauce and sesame seeds.
7. Serve a mound of rice on each plate with the stir-fried seafood and sauce spooned over. Scatter with coriander and serve with the remaining lime quarters.

Cauliflower, coconut & pea curry

Serves 4

➕ 450 calories

♥ 17.8g saturated fat

1 cauliflower, broken into small florets
1 tbsp ghee or coconut oil
1 onion, sliced
1 tsp ground cumin
1 tsp ground coriander
1 tbsp dried curry leaves
400ml (14fl oz) can coconut milk
150g (5½oz) peas, frozen or fresh
200g (7oz) chard or spinach, shredded
small bunch of coriander leaves,
    chopped
250g (9oz) ready-cooked basmati rice
salt and black pepper

To serve:
2 limes, halved (optional)
mango chutney

This is a super-quick curry yet full of fragrant spice flavours and enriched with coconut milk.

1. Steam the cauliflower for 3–4 minutes until just tender.
2. While the cauliflower is steaming, heat the ghee or coconut oil in a large saucepan, add the onion, spices, ½ teaspoon salt and black pepper to taste and fry over a high heat for 1 minute until the spices start to smell aromatic and the onion begins to colour.
3. Add the coconut milk and the steamed cauliflower and bring to the boil. Reduce the heat to a simmer, cover with a lid and cook for 5 minutes.
4. Add the peas and the shredded greens and taste for salt, adding more as necessary. Cook for a further 2 minutes for all the flavours to combine, then sprinkle with coriander.
5. Meanwhile, put the rice into a small saucepan with about a tablespoon of water over a high heat, cover and warm through for 2 minutes, stirring at intervals.
6. Serve on a bed of the rice with the lime halves on the side, if using, and the mango chutney.

Quinoa, salmon & vegetable bowl

Serves 2

➕ 667 calories

🔻 6.7g saturated fat

100g (3½oz) uncooked quinoa or
   150g (5½oz) ready-cooked quinoa
200ml (7fl oz) water
½ tsp salt
1 quantity Dressing for Grains
   (*see* page 186)
200g (7oz) sugarsnap peas
1 ripe avocado
50g (1¾oz) watercress, baby leaf
   spinach or rocket
150g (5½oz) roasted salmon slices
1 tbsp toasted sesame oil
1 tbsp sesame seeds, preferably
   toasted

This is a bowl of satisfaction that provides masses of nutrients for a healthy diet. For vegetarians, substitute the salmon with ramen eggs (*see* page 13).

1. Cook the quinoa with the measured water and salt as described on page 89.
2. While the quinoa is cooking, make the dressing (*see* page 186) and set aside.
3. Cook the sugarsnap peas in a saucepan of boiling water for 2 minutes. Drain and set aside.
4. Cut the avocado in half, remove the stone and peel, then slice the flesh.
5. When the quinoa is ready, drain in a sieve to remove any excess water and put it in a bowl. With your hands, tear the watercress or other leaves roughly and add to the quinoa with the dressing. Mix together well.
6. Divide the dressed quinoa between 2 bowls, lay the avocado slices, sugarsnaps and salmon slices decoratively around the edge and sprinkle with the sesame oil and sesame seeds.

Broccoli & smoked tofu with quinoa

Serves 2

➕ 643 calories

➖ 5.5g saturated fat

100g (3½oz) uncooked quinoa

200ml (7fl oz) water

½ tsp salt

3 tbsp vegetable oil

200g (7oz) smoked tofu, cut into
1cm (½-inch) cubes

1 garlic clove, thinly sliced

1 hot red chilli, deseeded and
finely chopped

a thumb-sized piece of fresh root
ginger (about 20g/¾oz), peeled
and finely chopped

1 tbsp pumpkin seeds

1 tbsp sunflower seeds

150g (5½oz) tenderstem broccoli

3 tbsp soy sauce

2 tbsp toasted sesame oil

Full of goodness, flavour and texture, this recipe makes a substantial, protein-rich vegetarian bowl. The broccoli and tofu are quickly stir-fried with ginger, chilli and soy-coated pumpkin and sunflower seeds for extra crunch, then tossed through a mound of steaming quinoa.

1. Cook the quinoa with the measured water and salt as described on page 89.
2. While the quinoa is cooking, heat 2 tablespoons of the oil in a wok until smoking hot. Pat the tofu dry with kitchen paper, add to the wok and fry over a high heat, turning and tossing, until the cubes are browned all over. Remove to a plate.
3. Heat the remaining tablespoon of oil in the wok, add the garlic, chilli and ginger and stir-fry over a medium–high heat for a few seconds. Add the pumpkin and sunflower seeds and fry for a few more seconds before adding the broccoli and 2 tablespoons of the soy sauce.
4. Cover the wok with a lid and steam for a couple of minutes until the broccoli is still firm but no longer raw.
5. When the quinoa is ready, drain in a sieve to remove any excess water. Remove the wok from the heat and add the quinoa with the remaining soy sauce and the sesame oil. Toss well before serving.

Variation: try making this with spelt, couscous or millet grain, which both have a similar texture to quinoa.

Teriyaki vegetable & rice bowl

Serves 4

➕ 409 calories

➖ 0.9g saturated fat

300g (10½oz) uncooked basmati
    or other long-grain white rice

¼ tsp salt

1 quantity Ginger Teriyaki Sauce
    (*see* page 187)

1 red or yellow pepper, cored,
    deseeded and thinly sliced

1 sweet potato, peeled and cut
    into chips

2 courgettes, cut into 5mm
    (¼-inch) slices

½ red cabbage, shredded

2 large handfuls of baby leaf spinach

1 tbsp toasted sesame oil

1 tbsp sesame seeds, preferably
    toasted (optional)

This ginger teriyaki sauce is a great way to give simple vegetables a real lift. Make extra and enjoy it in Teriyaki Chicken Potsu on page 90 as well, or use it in place of bottled teriyaki sauce for the Teriyaki Salmon & Ginger Rice on page 114.

1. Cook the rice with the salt as described on page 88.
2. While the rice is cooking, make the ginger teriyaki sauce (*see* page 187).
3. Steam or boil the red or yellow pepper and sweet potato together for 2 minutes, then add the courgettes and cook for 1 minute. Add the cabbage and then the spinach to cook for a final minute.
4. Drain the cooked vegetables, if necessary, and transfer to a bowl. Dress with the sesame oil and the sauce.
5. Divide the cooked rice between bowls and pile the vegetables on top. Sprinkle with the sesame seeds to serve, if you like.

Rice & lentils (kitchari)

Serves 2

➕ 527 calories

🔻 12.5g saturated fat

1 coconut oil, ghee or vegetable oil
2 tsp ginger paste
1 tsp garlic paste
1 tbsp dried curry leaves
1 tsp ground cumin
1 tsp ground coriander
1 tsp ground turmeric
40g (1½oz) creamed coconut, broken
    into pieces
250g (9oz) canned brown lentils
    (or use any ready-cooked lentils)
250g (9oz) ready-cooked rice
½ tsp salt
250ml (9fl oz) water
grated zest and juice of ½ lime

To serve:

10g (¼oz) coriander, roughly chopped
2 lime wedges

This is comfort food of the healthy kind, as it is both nourishing and cleansing. And by using ready-cooked lentils and rice, it can be made in next to no time.

1. Heat the oil or ghee in a large saucepan, add the ginger and garlic pastes and curry leaves and stir to coat in the oil or ghee. Fry briefly over a medium–high heat before adding the ground spices and coconut.
2. Reduce the heat to low and continue to stir so that the coconut melts into the oil or ghee and spices.
3. Add the lentils, rice, salt and measured water. Stir well and increase the heat so that the mixture just starts to boil and the water becomes absorbed.
4. Once the mixture has boiled, turn off the heat and add the lime zest and juice.
5. Sprinkle with the chopped coriander and serve each dish with a lime wedge, for squeezing over.

Variations: serve the dish Indian style with a dollop of natural yogurt and warm chapatis, or try using different rices and grains, such as ready-cooked brown basmati or quinoa, or ready-cooked or canned chickpeas. You can also add chopped, cooked spinach or other green vegetables at the end.

Edamame & quinoa salad

Serves 2

⊕ 477 calories

⊖ 0.7g saturated fat

200g (7oz) uncooked quinoa
400ml (14fl oz) water
100g (3½oz) edamame (soya) beans
    or peas, frozen or fresh
½ cucumber, cut into small chunks
1 large carrot, cut into long thin strips
    or strands with a julienne peeler
    or spiralizer
2 spring onions, finely chopped
100g (3½oz) cherry tomatoes, halved
1 quantity Thai Salad Dressing (*see*
    page 186), but made with green
    chilli in place of the red chilli
10g (¼oz) coriander, roughly chopped
salt

Alive with colour, this quick, nutritious salad can be prepared with other whole grains for variety – try millet, amaranth or spelt.

1. Cook the quinoa with the measured water and ¼ teaspoon of salt as described on page 89.
2. While the quinoa is cooking, cook the edamame beans or peas in a saucepan of salted boiling water for 2 minutes, then drain and refresh under cold running water. Prepare the salad vegetables.
3. Make the Thai salad dressing (*see* page 186).
4. When the quinoa is cooked, refresh under cold running water and drain well.
5. Mix the quinoa with the salad vegetables and coriander and stir in the dressing before serving.

Ginger beef with tofu

Serves 2

⊕ 517 calories

♥ 7.3g saturated fat

100g (3½oz) uncooked Japanese-style
    short-grain white rice
150ml (¼ pint) water
pinch of salt
2 tbsp groundnut or vegetable oil
1 hot green chilli, chopped
1 white onion, sliced
1 garlic clove, sliced
10g (¼oz) fresh root ginger, peeled
    and cut into fine sticks
200g (7oz) minced beef
1 tbsp soy sauce
1 tbsp oyster sauce
1 tbsp Shaoxing wine or dry sherry
50g (1¾oz) firm tofu, cut into 1cm
    (½-inch) cubes
1 hot red chilli, chopped, to serve

**Made with storecupboard ingredients, this stir-fry is
perfect for an easy and filling after-work supper.**

1. Cook the rice with the measured water and salt as
   described on page 88.
2. While the rice is cooking, prepare all the other ingredients
   and place them next to the hob so that they are close at
   hand when you start to stir-fry.
3. Heat 1 tablespoon of the oil in a wok, add the chilli and
   stir-fry over a medium–high heat for a few seconds. Add
   the onion and stir-fry for 1 minute until it starts to soften,
   then add the garlic and ginger and stir-fry for a further
   minute to just colour. Remove to a plate and set aside.
4. Heat the remaining tablespoon of oil in the wok, add the
   minced beef and fry over a high heat for about 1 minute,
   breaking up any lumps, until it starts to colour. If it releases
   any water, continue frying until it evaporates and the beef
   starts to colour.
5. Add the soy and oyster sauces and the Shaoxing wine or
   sherry, then return the onion mixture to the wok, tossing
   and coating it all. Finally, add the tofu cubes and carefully
   stir-fry to heat through.
6. Serve on the cooked rice, with the red chilli scattered over
   for a splash of colour.

Five-spice pork with hoisin on sticky rice

Serves 2

- 682 calories
- 7.4g saturated fat

150g (5½oz) uncooked Japanese-style
    short-grain white rice
200ml (7fl oz) water
200g (7oz) pork fillet, cut into 5mm
    (¼-inch) slices
1 tsp Chinese five-spice powder
2 tbsp groundnut oil
1 garlic clove, sliced
1 hot red chilli, chopped
a thumb-sized piece of fresh root
    ginger (about 20g/¾oz), peeled
    and sliced
2 spring onions, finely chopped
100g (3½oz) white cabbage, shredded
100g (3½oz) spring greens, shredded
100g (3½oz) mangetout
2 tbsp soy sauce
1 tbsp hoisin sauce
1 tbsp Shaoxing wine or dry sherry
1 tbsp rice vinegar
salt

Chinese five-spice powder and hoisin work their magic with pork to create this tasty stir-fried dish.

1. Cook the rice with the measured water and a pinch of salt as described on page 88.
2. While the rice is cooking, put the pork slices in a bowl with the five-spice and a pinch of salt and toss to coat.
3. Prepare all the other ingredients and place them next to the hob so that they are close at hand when you start to stir-fry.
4. Heat 1 tablespoon of the oil in a wok until smoking. Add the pork and stir-fry over a high heat for about 30 seconds until it turns from pink to brown. Remove to a plate and set aside.
5. Heat another tablespoon of the oil in the wok, add the garlic, chilli and ginger and stir-fry over a medium–high heat for about 30 seconds until the garlic starts to colour.
6. Add the spring onions to the wok and stir-fry for a few minutes, then add the cabbage and cook for 30 seconds.
7. Add the spring greens and mangetout to the wok and cook for a further minute, then add the soy sauce and toss well. Remove to a warm plate.
8. Return the pork to the wok with the hoisin sauce, and when it is bubbling, add the Shaoxing wine or sherry and rice vinegar to make a sauce. Turn off the heat.
9. Divide the rice between 2 plates and top with the pork and sauce, then serve with the vegetables alongside.

soups

Chicken & sweetcorn soup

Serves 2

● 431 calories

● 3.25g saturated fat

1 tbsp toasted sesame oil

2 spring onions, roughly chopped

1 tbsp ginger paste

1 hot red chilli, deseeded and
    roughly chopped

600g (1lb 5oz) canned sweetcorn

700ml (1¼ pints) ready-made chicken
    stock (*see* page 180)

¼ tsp salt

1 tsp cornflour or potato flour

2 tbsp sake or dry sherry

1 free-range egg, lightly beaten

100g (3½oz) cooked chicken
    breast slices

10g (¼oz) coriander, roughly
    chopped

**This favourite soup is so simple to prepare and makes
creative use of any leftover cooked chicken.**

1. Heat the oil in a large saucepan, add the spring onions,
   ginger paste and chilli and fry over a medium–high heat
   for about 30 seconds.
2. Set aside 2 tablespoons of the sweetcorn for later and
   add the remainder to the saucepan with the stock and salt.
   Cover with a lid and bring to the boil over a high heat.
3. Put the cornflour or potato flour into a cup or small bowl
   and mix with the sake or sherry to a smooth paste, then
   add to the boiling stock and cook, stirring, for 2 minutes.
4. Blend the mixture with a stick blender or in a jug blender
   until completely smooth. Rinse the saucepan and push the
   blended mixture through a sieve back into it, using the back
   of a spoon to push as much liquid as you can through the
   sieve. You may need to do this in a couple of batches, but
   make sure you discard the solids from the sieve as you go.
5. Bring the soup back to the boil and slowly pour in the
   beaten egg, stirring as you go. As it boils, thin strands
   of cooked egg will appear in the soup.
6. Add the chicken, the reserved sweetcorn and the
   coriander and heat through before serving.

Chicken katsu soup

Serves 4

⊕ 367 calories

⊖ 6.2g saturated fat

2 tbsp vegetable or groundnut oil
2 tsp ginger paste
1 tsp garlic paste
1 tsp chilli flakes
4 spring onions, finely chopped
400g (14oz) peeled and deseeded
    butternut squash or sweet potato,
    cut into 1cm (½-inch) chunks or
    grated in a food processor
½ tsp Chinese five-spice powder
½ tsp ground turmeric
3½ tbsp soy sauce, plus extra to serve
170ml (6fl oz) single cream
200ml (7fl oz) boiling water
500ml (18fl oz) ready-made light
    chicken stock (*see* page 180)
300g (10½oz) cooked chicken
    breast slices
200g (7oz) frozen edamame
    (soya) beans

This Japanese curry-style sauce makes a delicious and unusual soup base.

1. Heat the oil in a large saucepan, add the ginger and garlic pastes and chilli flakes and fry over a medium–high heat for about 30 seconds.
2. Add the spring onions, squash or sweet potato and spices and fry together for a minute, then add the soy sauce and cook for a further minute before adding the cream, measured boiling water and the stock.
3. Bring the mixture to the boil and cook for 10 minutes until the squash or sweet potato is completely tender.
4. Blend the mixture with a stick blender or in a jug blender until smooth.
5. Return to the saucepan, bring back to the boil and add the chicken and edamame beans. Simmer for 2 minutes until the beans are cooked.
6. Serve with extra soy sauce at the table.

Thai green chicken & squash soup

Serves 4

⊕ 159 calories

⊖ 2.7g saturated fat

1 tbsp coconut oil, ghee or vegetable oil

1 tsp garlic paste

1 tsp ginger paste

1 hot red or green chilli, deseeded and roughly chopped

½ lemon grass stalk, roughly chopped

2 dried lime leaves, roughly chopped

4 tbsp or 48g (1¾oz) packet Thai green curry paste

400g (14oz) peeled and deseeded butternut squash, cut into 1cm (½-inch) chunks or grated in a food processor

800ml (1⅓ pints) boiling water

250g (9oz) boneless, skinless chicken breast, cut into bite-sized pieces

10g (¼oz) coriander, roughly chopped

juice of 1 lime

salt and black pepper

If you can't find butternut squash, try using sweet potato or experiment by adding your favourite greens.

1. Heat the oil in a large saucepan, add the garlic and ginger pastes, chilli, lemon grass and lime leaves and fry over a medium–high heat for about 30 seconds.
2. Add the curry paste and continue to fry for about 1 minute.
3. Add the squash and stir well so that it is coated in the curry mixture and starts to fry.
4. Pour the measured boiling water over the squash, cover the pan with a lid and cook, at a gentle boil, for about 7 minutes, or until the squash is tender.
5. Blend the soup with a stick blender or in a jug blender until smooth.
6. Return the soup to the saucepan, season to taste with salt and black pepper and bring it back to the boil.
7. Add the chicken pieces and cook for 1 minute, or until they turn opaque and are cooked through.
8. Stir in the coriander and lime juice before serving.

Detox chicken & vegetable soup

Serves 4

⊕ 170 calories

⊗ 0.4g saturated fat

200g (7oz) boneless, skinless chicken
    breast, cut into thin slices

2 tbsp soy sauce

1.5 litres (2¾ pints) ready-made
    chicken stock (*see* page 180)

1 red chilli, chopped

1 tbsp ginger paste

½ tsp ground fennel

½ tsp ground coriander

3 carrots (about 220g/7¾oz),
    finely chopped

100g (3½oz) shiitake or chestnut
    mushrooms, chopped

1 leek, trimmed, cleaned and
    thinly sliced

½ white cabbage, thinly sliced

100g (3½oz) green beans, topped
    and cut into short lengths

¼ tsp salt, plus extra if needed

black pepper

Clean, fresh-tasting and packed with vegetables, this is a nourishing soup for those healthier days.

1. Put the chicken slices into a bowl with the soy sauce and toss to coat. Set aside.
2. Bring the stock to the boil in a large saucepan while you prepare the other ingredients.
3. Add all the remaining ingredients to the boiling stock and simmer for 4–5 minutes, then add the chicken pieces and soy sauce and continue to cook for a further minute until the chicken is opaque and cooked through.
4. Add extra seasoning to taste, if needed, before serving.

Prawn, tamarind & chilli soup

Serves 2

➕ 180 calories

❤ 0.3g saturated fat

100g (3½oz) chestnut or shiitake
  mushrooms, sliced
2 heads of pak choi, about 200g
  (7oz), stalks and leaves separated
  and sliced
150g (5½oz) cooked peeled prawns
juice of ½ lime
10g (¼oz) coriander, roughly chopped
2 spring onions, roughly chopped

For the broth:
800ml (1⅓ pints) ready-made chicken
  stock (*see* page 180)
1 hot red chilli, finely chopped
1 lemon grass stalk, finely chopped
10g (¼oz) fresh root ginger, peeled
  and sliced
1 tbsp fish sauce
1 tbsp tamarind paste
2 tsp agave syrup

**This is a super-simple soup but full of zingy flavours –
sweet, sour, hot and fragrant – along with juicy bites
of prawn.**

1. To make the broth, put the stock with all the other broth
   ingredients into a large saucepan and bring to the boil, then
   reduce the heat and simmer for 5 minutes or so to allow the
   flavours to infuse while you prepare the other ingredients.
2. Add the mushrooms to the broth and bring to a gentle
   boil. Cook for a couple of minutes, then add the pak choi
   stalks and cook for a further minute.
3. Add the prawns and the pak choi leaves and continue
   to cook for a further minute, just so that the prawns heat
   through and the leaves wilt.
4. Divide the soup between 2 bowls and sprinkle the lime
   juice, coriander and spring onions over each before serving.

Salmon & asparagus miso

Serves 2

⊕ 110 calories

⬤ 1.7g saturated fat

800ml (1⅓ pints) boiling water

2 tbsp miso paste

1 tbsp soy sauce

150g (5½oz) asparagus spears, cut into short lengths

150g (5½oz) skinned salmon fillet, cut into 1cm (½-inch) pieces

100g (3½oz) bean sprouts

1 sheet of nori (optional)

If you can't find miso paste, buy sachets of instant miso soup instead. Try experimenting with other green vegetables: peas, edamame (soya) beans or broad beans are all great alternatives.

1. Pour the measured boiling water into a large saucepan.
2. Put the miso in a cup or small bowl and mix with a tablespoon of the boiling water to soften it slightly and make a smooth liquid paste, then whisk into the pan of water along with the soy sauce to combine.
3. Bring the miso broth to the boil, add the asparagus and cook for 2 minutes.
4. Add the salmon and cook for a further minute, then stir in the bean sprouts.
5. Spoon the fish and vegetables into 2 bowls and pour the miso broth over the top.
6. Cut the sheet of nori into small shreds with kitchen scissors and scatter over each bowl to serve, if you like.

Crab & sweetcorn soup

Serves 2

- 432 calories
- 2.9g saturated fat

1 tbsp groundnut or vegetable oil
4 spring onions, roughly chopped
a thumb-sized piece of fresh root
    ginger (about 20g/¾oz), peeled
    and roughly chopped
1 hot red chilli, deseeded or seeds left
    in depending on how hot you like
    it, roughly chopped
650g (1lb 7oz) canned sweetcorn
800ml (1⅓ pints) boiling water
1 tsp salt
1 tsp cornflour or potato flour
2 tbsp sake or dry sherry
100g (3½oz) cooked white crabmeat
10g (¼oz) coriander, roughly chopped
1 tbsp toasted sesame oil
black pepper

Lighter and fresher than the ubiquitous version served in Chinese restaurants, this soup is full of flavour and yet quick to prepare.

1. Heat the groundnut or vegetable oil in a large saucepan, add the spring onions, ginger and chilli and fry over a medium–high heat for about 30 seconds.
2. Set aside 50g (1¾oz) of the sweetcorn and add the remainder to the saucepan with the measured boiling water and salt.
3. Put the cornflour or potato flour into a cup or small bowl and mix with the sake or sherry to a smooth paste, then add to the boiling water and cook, stirring, for 2 minutes.
4. Blend the mixture with a stick blender or in a jug blender until completely smooth. Rinse the saucepan and push the blended mixture through a sieve back into it, using the back of a spoon to push as much liquid as you can through the sieve. You may need to do this in a couple of batches, but make sure you discard the solids from the sieve as you go.
5. Bring the soup back to the boil and add the crabmeat, the reserved sweetcorn, the coriander and black pepper to taste. Heat through for a minute, then stir in the sesame oil before serving.

Sweet potato & crispy kale soup

Serves 2

➕ 447 calories

🔻 5.3g saturated fat

3 tbsp groundnut oil

1 onion, chopped

1 garlic clove, chopped

10g (¼oz) fresh root ginger, peeled
   and sliced

2 sweet potatoes, peeled and
   chopped, or 250g (9oz) ready-
   prepared diced sweet potato

1 tsp chilli flakes

1 chicken stock cube or concentrated
   jellied stock, such as Knorr Chicken
   Stock Pot

800ml (1⅓ pints) boiling water

100g (3½oz) curly kale, tough stalks
   removed

25g (1oz) cashew nuts, roughly
   chopped

salt and black pepper

Sweet potato cooks quicker than most root vegetables, so it is ideal to use for a speedy soup, and you can buy it ready-diced to make preparation even faster. The crispy kale and crunchy nuts provide a nice contrast to the smooth soup.

1. Heat 2 tablespoons of the oil in a large saucepan, add the onion, garlic and ginger and fry over a medium–high heat for 1 minute until just starting to colour.

2. Add the sweet potatoes, chilli flakes, stock cube or jellied stock and measured boiling water, season with ½ teaspoon salt and black pepper to taste and bring to the boil.

3. Cover with a lid and boil for 10 minutes, stirring occasionally.

4. Meanwhile, heat the remaining tablespoon of oil in a wok until smoking hot. Add the kale and a pinch of salt and stir-fry over a high heat for 2–3 minutes until it starts to smell toasted and the leaves are crisp.

5. Blend the soup with a stick blender or in a jug blender until smooth, then ladle into bowls and scatter with the crispy kale and cashew nuts to serve.

Prawn & coconut soup

Serves 2

- 351 calories
- 16.3g saturated fat

1 tbsp vegetable or groundnut oil
1 hot red chilli, deseeded and chopped
1 garlic clove, chopped
a small knob of fresh root ginger,
    peeled and grated
½ lemon grass stalk, finely chopped
½ x 400ml (14fl oz) can coconut milk
800ml (1⅓ pints) ready-made fish stock
    (*see* page 180)
¼ tsp salt
2 heads of pak choi
150g (5½oz) cooked peeled prawns
juice of 1 lime
10g (¼oz) bunch of coriander, chopped

Frozen prawns work well and you can now buy good-quality, ready-made fish stock from small supermarkets. Try to use fresh lemon grass if you can; any left over keeps well in the freezer for later use.

1. Heat the oil in a large saucepan, add the chilli, garlic, ginger and lemon grass and fry over a medium–high heat for 1 minute until they just start to colour.
2. Add the coconut milk, fish stock and salt and bring to the boil.
3. While the stock is coming to the boil, separate the stalks and leaves of the pak choi and cut the stalks into slices and shred the leaves.
4. Add the pak choi stalks and the prawns to the stock once it is boiling and cook for 2 minutes.
5. Turn off the heat and add the shredded pak choi leaves, the lime juice and the coriander before serving.

Squid & tofu tom yum

Serves 2

⊕ 251 calories

⊖ 1.2g saturated fat

100g (3½oz) enoki (enokitake) or straw
    mushrooms, or chestnut or button
    mushrooms, thinly sliced

150g (5½oz) firm tofu, cut into 1cm
    (½-inch) cubes

150g (5½oz) squid rings

100g (3½oz) cherry tomatoes, halved

10g (¼oz) mixed basil and coriander
    leaves

For the broth:

800ml (1⅓ pints) ready-made chicken
    stock (*see page 180*)

1 shallot, thinly sliced

a thumb-sized piece of fresh root
    ginger (about 20g/¾oz), peeled
    and finely chopped

4 dried lime leaves, crumbled or
    chopped

1 hot red chilli, chopped

2 tbsp fish sauce

1 tbsp agave syrup or palm sugar

The classic tom yum flavours of hot, sour, salty and sweet infuse into the tofu and squid. If squid isn't available, you can use uncooked prawns instead.

1. To make the broth, put the stock with all the other broth ingredients into a large saucepan and bring to the boil, then reduce the heat and simmer for 5 minutes.
2. Add the mushrooms to the simmering broth and cook for 3 minutes, before adding the tofu and squid rings.
3. Bring to the boil, then turn off the heat. Add the tomatoes and leave for 1 minute to allow them to soften.
4. Divide the soup between 2 bowls and tear the basil and coriander leaves over before serving.

Hot–sour pork & mushroom soup

Serves 2

⊕ 243 calories

⊖ 2.2g saturated fat

100g (3½oz) chestnut or button
    mushrooms, thinly sliced
150g (5½oz) leftover cooked pork
    or uncooked pork loin, cut into
    small cubes
4 spring onions, chopped
2 tbsp lime juice

For the broth:
800ml (1⅓ pints) ready-made chicken
    stock (*see page 180*)
30g (1oz) fresh root ginger, peeled
    and sliced
1 lemon grass stalk, chopped
4 dried lime leaves
2 tbsp lime juice
2 tbsp fish sauce
1 tbsp palm sugar or agave syrup
1–2 tsp chilli flakes, or to taste
¼ tsp salt
20g (¾oz) bunch of coriander, stalks
    and leaves
lime wedges, to serve

**This is perfect for using up pork left over from a roast –
or use chicken as an alternative – but otherwise buy pork
loin, as it is very lean.**

1. To make the broth, put the stock with all the other broth
   ingredients into a large saucepan (start with 1 teaspoon
   chilli flakes and increase the amount later if you want more
   heat). Chop the coriander stalks off the bunch, keeping
   them tied together so that you can fish them out later
   (reserve the leaves for serving), and add to the pan. Cover
   with a lid and bring to the boil.
2. Cook at a gentle boil for 8 minutes for the flavours to
   infuse, then strain, discarding the solids, and return to
   the saucepan.
3. Bring the broth back to the boil and add the mushrooms.
   Re-cover and boil for 3 minutes until tender.
4. Add the pork and cook for a further 2–3 minutes until
   heated through, or just cooked through if using uncooked
   loin. Then add the spring onions, lime juice and more chilli
   to taste if you like.
5. Sprinkle with the reserved coriander leaves and serve with
   lime wedges.

Sweet potato, tamarind & coconut soup

Serves 4

➕ 438 calories

🔻 16.6g saturated fat with vegetable oil
(21g saturated fat with coconut oil)

2 tbsp coconut or vegetable oil
2 onions, finely chopped
½ tsp salt, plus extra if needed
4 sweet potatoes, peeled and cut
    into 1cm (½-inch) cubes
2 hot red chillies, deseeded and
    finely chopped
4 dried lime leaves
400ml (14fl oz) can coconut milk
600ml (20fl oz) water
4 tbsp tamarind paste
juice of 1 lime
black pepper

To serve (optional):
toasted pumpkin seeds and/or sunflower
    seeds and flaked coconut
lime slices

This luxurious, velvety soup has great flavour balance – sweet notes from the sweet potato, sour from the tamarind and richness from the coconut – with the simple ingredients working together to create something really special. Topping it with the toasted seeds and flaked coconut provides a pleasing crunchy contrast.

1. Heat the oil in a large saucepan, add the onions with the salt and fry over a high heat for a couple of minutes.
2. Add the sweet potatoes, chillies, lime leaves, coconut milk, measured water and tamarind paste. Give everything a good stir, bring to the boil and cook for 10–15 minutes until the sweet potato is tender.
3. Remove the lime leaves and blend the soup with a stick blender or in a jug blender. Season with extra salt, if needed, black pepper to taste and the lime juice.
4. Pour the soup into bowls and serve sprinkled with toasted pumpkin and/or sunflower seeds and flaked coconut and accompanied by lime slices, if you like.

Root vegetable miso

Serves 2

⊕ 188 calories

♥ 0.8g saturated fat

800ml (1⅓ pints) boiling water

2 tbsp miso paste

2 tbsp soy sauce, plus extra to taste, if needed

1 swede, about 200g (7oz), peeled and cut into 1cm (½-inch) cubes

1 parsnip, about 150g (5½oz), peeled and cut into 1cm (½-inch) cubes

2 carrots, about 200g (7oz), cut into 1cm (½-inch) cubes

2 spring onions, chopped

100g (3½oz) firm tofu, cut into 1cm (½-inch) cubes

The earthy flavours of root vegetables work well with miso, and tofu adds healthy protein. Buy packets of ready-cut root vegetable assortments to make this a super-quick, sustaining supper.

1. Pour the measured boiling water into a large saucepan.
2. Put the miso in a cup or small bowl and mix with a tablespoon of the boiling water to soften it slightly and make a smooth liquid paste, then whisk into the pan of water along with the soy sauce to combine.
3. Add the root vegetable pieces to the miso broth and bring to a simmer. Cook for 10–12 minutes until tender.
4. Taste for salt, adding more soy if necessary, and finally add the spring onions and tofu to heat through before serving.

Time-saving tip: the smaller you cut the root vegetables, the quicker they will cook.

Shiitake & sweet potato soup

Serves 2

➕ 351 calories

➖ 2.6g saturated fat

800ml (1⅓ pints) ready-made chicken
    stock (*see* page 180 – but don't use
    a stock cube)
20g (¾oz) bunch of coriander, stalks
    and leaves
1 tsp ginger paste
1 hot red chilli, deseeded and finely
    chopped
3 dried lime leaves, shredded
1 tbsp fish sauce
100g (3½oz) shiitake or chestnut
    mushrooms, sliced
2 sweet potatoes, peeled and cut into
    1cm (½-inch) cubes
handful of spinach, shredded
1 lime

To serve:

100g (3½oz) firm tofu, cut into 1cm
    (½-inch) cubes, or 2 poached
    free-range eggs
1 tbsp black and white sesame seeds,
    preferably toasted

**A few storecupboard ingredients can make the world
of difference to a simple stock, then just add fresh
vegetables and you have a delicious soup created
with no fuss.**

1. Put the chicken stock into a large saucepan with the
   stalks cut from the bunch of coriander, keeping them
   tied together so that you can fish them out later. Add the
   ginger paste, chilli, lime leaves and fish sauce and bring
   the stock to the boil.
2. While you are waiting for the stock to come up to the boil,
   prepare the vegetables.
3. Add the mushrooms and sweet potatoes to the boiling
   stock and cook for 5 minutes. Then add the spinach and
   cook for a further minute.
4. Remove the coriander stalks. Grate a few strokes of lime
   zest into the broth, then taste the broth and squeeze half
   of the lime into it. Taste it again and add more lime juice
   to taste.
5. Serve with the tofu cubes or a poached egg in each bowl,
   for extra protein, and garnish with sesame seeds.

Cleansing Asian vegetable broth

Serves 2

⊕ 170 calories

♥ 0.4g saturated fat

3 or 4 of the following (or anything else that takes your fancy!):

100g (3½oz) ready-prepared diced sweet potato

1 leek, trimmed, cleaned and sliced

100g (3½oz) curly kale, tough stalks removed, torn into small pieces

100g (3½oz) green beans, topped and cut into thirds

100g (3½oz) baby corn, cut into thirds

1 head of pak choi, stalks and leaves separated and sliced

100g (3½oz) spinach

grated zest and juice of ½ lime

For the broth:

800ml (1 pint) ready-made vegetable stock (*see* page 180)

1 star anise

4 large dried lime leaves

1 lemon grass stalk, finely chopped

a thumb-sized piece of fresh root ginger (about 20g/¾oz), peeled and finely chopped

1 hot red chilli, finely chopped

4 spring onions, finely chopped

¼ tsp salt

Get the broth bubbling and the flavours infusing while you cut up some vegetables. Then drop them into the boiling broth as you go, adding the ones that take longer to cook first.

1. To make the broth, put the stock with all the other broth ingredients into a large saucepan, cover with a lid and bring to the boil.
2. While you are waiting for the broth to come up to the boil, prepare the vegetables.
3. Add the vegetables to the boiling broth in the order in which they will take time to cook.
4. Finish with the lime zest and juice before serving.

Green curry soup with cauliflower & peas

Serves 2

⊕ 326 calories

♥ 10g saturated fat

1 tbsp ghee, coconut or vegetable oil

1 hot red or green chilli, deseeded and
   roughly chopped

1 tsp ginger paste

½ lemon grass stalk, roughly chopped

4 dried lime leaves, roughly chopped

4 tbsp or 48g (1¾oz) packet Thai green
   curry paste

1 tbsp creamed coconut

600g (1lb 5oz) cauliflower, cut into
   small florets, or ready-prepared
   cauliflower florets

800ml (1⅓ pints) boiling water

½ tsp salt

150g (5½oz) peas or edamame (soya)
   beans, frozen or fresh

10g (¼oz) coriander, roughly chopped

juice of 1 lime

The fragrant flavours of green curry add a boost to simple vegetables to create an exotic-tasting soup. You can buy ready-cut cauliflower florets in the supermarket to make prepping even quicker.

1. Heat the ghee or oil in a large saucepan, add the chilli, ginger paste, lemon grass, lime leaves and curry paste and fry over a medium–high heat for about 1 minute.

2. Add the creamed coconut, cauliflower, measured boiling water and salt, cover with a lid and cook at a gentle boil for 8 minutes, or until the cauliflower is tender.

3. Blend the soup with a stick blender or in a jug blender until smooth and return to the saucepan, if necessary.

4. Bring the soup back to the boil. Add the peas or beans and cook for 1 minute, then stir in the coriander and lime juice before serving.

Nourishing broth with ginger, mushrooms & greens

Serves 2

➕ 232 calories

♥ 0.5g saturated fat

1 litre (1¾ pints) ready-made chicken stock (*see* page 180)

2 boneless, skinless chicken thighs, cut into bite-sized pieces

2 hot red chillies, deseeded and sliced

2 tbsp ginger paste

2 tbsp miso paste

1 tbsp soy sauce

50g (1¾oz) enoki (enokitake) or straw mushrooms

1 bunch of curly kale or spring greens, tough stalks removed, finely shredded

2 carrots, sliced or cut into long thin strips with a julienne peeler

1 tbsp nigella seeds, to serve

Cooking the chicken thigh meat in the stock saves time and also gives the broth extra flavour and nourishment.

1. Pour the stock into a large saucepan, add the chicken, chillies and ginger paste and bring to the boil. Reduce the heat slightly and cook for 12 minutes while you prepare the vegetables.

2. Add the miso and soy sauce to the stock with the mushrooms and kale or spring greens and cook for 3 minutes, then add the carrots and cook for a further 2 minutes.

3. Divide the broth between 2 bowls and sprinkle the nigella seeds on top before serving.

Seven-vegetable soup with rice

Serves 4

➕ 289 calories

🔽 1.6g saturated fat

1 red onion, peeled
2 leeks, trimmed and cleaned
150g (5½oz) mushrooms (*see* page 10)
2 tbsp groundnut oil
1 tsp ground turmeric
½ tsp salt, plus extra to taste, if needed
150g (5½oz) uncooked long-grain
    white rice (or a white basmati and
    wild rice mixture that cooks in
    under 20 minutes)
2 vegetable or chicken stock cubes,
    crumbled
1 courgette, cut into 1cm (½-inch)
    chunks
1.5 litres (2¾ pints) boiling water
100g (3½oz) spring greens, shredded
150g (5½oz) frozen edamame (soya)
    beans or peas
juice of ½ lemon
black pepper

Using a food processor to cut up some of the vegetables makes this soup even speedier to prepare. It is packed with healthy greens and the turmeric has anti-inflammatory qualities to give your body a beneficial boost.

1. Chop the onion, leeks and mushrooms into small pieces in a food processor.
2. Heat the oil in a large saucepan and add the chopped vegetable mixture from the food processor, turmeric, salt and black pepper to taste. Stir well, cover and cook for a couple of minutes over a medium–high heat while you prepare the remaining vegetables.
3. Add the rice, stock cubes and courgette to the pan, then pour in the measured boiling water. Bring to the boil, cover and cook for 10 minutes (or according to the packet instructions if using a white and wild rice mixture).
4. Add the spring greens and beans or peas and cook for a further 2–3 minutes until tender.
5. Taste the broth, adding more salt if necessary, and squeeze over the lemon juice before serving.

Vegetable miso & poached egg

Serves 2

● 204 calories

♥ 3.4g saturated fat

800ml (1⅓ pints) ready-made
    vegetable stock (*see* page 180)

4 tbsp soy sauce

2 tbsp miso paste

2 carrots, cut into long thin strands or
    strips with a spiralizer or julienne
    peeler, or grated

100g (3½oz) mangetout or
    sugarsnap peas

100g (3½oz) spring greens or cabbage,
    thinly sliced

2 free-range eggs

50g (1¾oz) firm tofu, smoked or plain,
    cut into 1cm (½-inch) cubes

2 tbsp black and white sesame seeds,
    preferably toasted

Perfect for a meat-free diet, this soup provides plenty of protein from the egg and tofu as well as loads of nutritious vegetables. If you have a spiralizer, this is a great way to prepare the vegetables here, but otherwise use a handy julienne peeler to create long thin strips that will cook equally quickly.

1. Put the vegetable stock into a large saucepan and bring to the boil.
2. For poaching the eggs, fill a separate saucepan with boiling water and add 1 tablespoon of the soy sauce. Bring to a simmer.
3. Put the miso in a cup or small bowl and mix with remaining soy sauce to soften it slightly and make a smooth liquid paste, then whisk into the boiling stock to combine.
4. Add all the vegetables to the broth and cook them for 2–3 minutes.
5. While the vegetables are cooking, crack each egg in turn into a cup, then gently slip into the simmering water and poach for 3 minutes. If you are not confident about poaching eggs, use an egg-poaching basket or lay 2 ring moulds about 6cm (2½ inches) in diameter on the base of the pan and drop an egg into each.
6. Scoop out the vegetables and divide between 2 bowls.
7. Put a poached egg into each bowl, on top of the vegetables, and pour the hot stock over. Add the tofu cubes and toasted sesame seeds before serving.

Super-green alkaline soup

Serves 4

➕ 142 calories

❤ 0.7g saturated fat

2 tbsp groundnut or vegetable oil

2 shallots, sliced

a thumb-sized piece of fresh root
  ginger (about 20g/¾oz), peeled
  and chopped

¼ tsp salt, plus extra to taste, if needed

2 courgettes, chopped

200g (7oz) frozen peas or a mixture
  of frozen peas and edamame
  (soya) beans

300g (10½oz) baby leaf spinach

1.5 litres (2¾ pints) boiling water

2 chicken or vegetable stock cubes

40g (1½oz) mixed basil, coriander and
  parsley with a few mint leaves,
  roughly chopped

juice of 1 lime

black pepper

Green vegetables and herbs are high-alkaline ingredients to keep your body in balance. If you like chilli, add a teaspoon of chilli flakes for an extra kick. Any leftovers are great eaten chilled too.

1. Heat the oil in a large saucepan, add the shallots, ginger and salt and fry over a medium–high heat for 1 minute.
2. Add the courgettes and fry for a further minute before adding the peas, or peas and beans, and spinach.
3. Pour over the measured boiling water and crumble in the stock cubes. Cover with a lid, bring to the boil and cook for 5–8 minutes until the courgettes are tender.
4. Add the herbs and lime juice, then taste for salt, adding more if needed, and add some black pepper.
5. Blend with a stick blender or in a jug blender until smooth before serving.

Using ready-made stocks

All sorts of ready-made stocks are now easily available to buy including chicken, vegetable, fish or beef stock cubes, concentrated jellied stocks (such as Knorr Stock Pots) and liquid sachets. They all have a great shelf life and can be stored for months in your cupboard, ready to use at any time.

The liquid stock varieties tend to be the cleanest tasting, so they are the best choice to use in recipes where the broth has relatively few added ingredients and flavourings. However, diluting a concentrated jellied stock or stock cube with boiling water can make preparation that much faster.

Ramen chicken miso broth

Serves 2
- 115 calories
- 0.7g saturated fat

1 litre (1¾ pints) ready-made chicken stock (*see* above)
a thumb-sized piece of fresh root ginger (about 20g/¾oz), peeled and sliced
1 hot red chilli, roughly chopped
4 spring onions, whole green tops only (reserve the white parts to garnish your dish)
2 tbsp miso paste
1 tbsp soy sauce
2 tsp sesame paste or tahini

1. Put the stock into a large saucepan with the ginger, chilli and green spring onion tops and bring to the boil. Reduce the heat and simmer for about 10 minutes to allow the flavours to infuse.
2. Put the miso in a cup or small bowl and mix with the soy sauce to soften it slightly and to make a

smooth liquid paste, then whisk into the broth with the sesame paste or tahini to combine.
3. Strain the broth, discarding the solids, and return to the pan to keep warm.

Variation: for **vegetable ramen broth**, use ready-made vegetable stock instead of chicken.

Seafood ramen broth

Serves 4
- 84 calories
- 0.1g saturated fat

1.5 litres (2¾ pints) ready-made fish stock (*see* above)
4 tbsp soy sauce
a thumb-sized piece of fresh root ginger (about 20g/¾oz), peeled and chopped
½ red onion, thinly sliced
4 carrots, cut into long thin strips or strands with a julienne peeler or spiralizer

1. Bring the fish stock to the boil in a large saucepan and add the remaining ingredients. Simmer for 3 minutes.

Walnut miso broth

Serves 4
- 118 calories
- 0.8g saturated fat

800ml (1⅓ pints) ready-made vegetable stock or chicken stock (*see* above)
100g (3½oz) shiitake, enoki (enokitake), oyster or chestnut mushrooms, or a mixture, halved or sliced if large
4 spring onions, finely chopped

For the walnut miso:
50g (1¾oz) ground walnuts
1 tbsp miso paste
2 tsp rice vinegar
1 tbsp soy sauce

Walnut miso broth *cont.*

1 tsp agave syrup or any brown sugar
1 tbsp water

1. Put the stock into a saucepan with the mushrooms and spring onions and bring to the boil, then reduce the heat and simmer while you prepare the walnut miso and any additional ingredients.
2. Put all the walnut miso ingredients into a jug and whizz to a smooth paste with a stick blender.
3. Stir the walnut miso into the simmering broth.

Variation: the walnut miso can also be used as a dressing for cooked chicken or steamed vegetables to serve with rice.

Vietnamese beef broth

Serves 4

➕ 27 calories
💙 trace saturated fat

800ml (1⅓ pints) ready-made beef stock (*see opposite*)
½ cinnamon stick
2 cloves
1 star anise
1 tsp fennel seeds
4 green cardamom pods
1 tsp coriander seeds
8 whole black peppercorns
a thumb-sized piece of fresh root ginger (about 20g/¾oz), peeled and cut into thick pieces
1 strip of orange rind
1 tsp agave syrup, palm sugar or any brown sugar
1 tsp fish sauce
20g (¾oz) bunch of coriander, stalks and leaves

1. Put all the ingredients except the coriander into a saucepan. Chop the coriander stalks off the bunch, keeping them tied together so that you can fish them out later (reserve the leaves to garnish your dish), and add to the pan. Bring to the boil, then reduce the heat and leave to

simmer for 10 minutes while you prepare any additional ingredients.
2. After the broth has simmered for 10 minutes, strain into a jug, discarding the solids, and return to the saucepan. Bring the broth back to the boil.

Variations: for **Vietnamese vegetable broth**, use ready-made vegetable stock in place of the beef stock and omit the orange rind; for **Vietnamese chicken broth**, use ready-made chicken stock instead and again omit the orange rind.

Vietnamese fish broth

Serves 4

➕ 35 calories
💙 trace saturated fat

800ml (1⅓ pints) ready-made fish stock (Waitrose do a good ready-made fish stock, or use 1 Knorr Fish Stock Pot diluted with water)
1 tbsp coriander seeds
1 star anise
1 tbsp fennel seeds
1 lemon grass stalk, chopped into small pieces
2 dried lime leaves
a thumb-sized piece of fresh root ginger (about 20g/¾oz), peeled and grated
1 hot red chilli, seeds in, halved
2 tsp coconut sugar, palm sugar or any brown sugar
2 tsp fish sauce
20g (¾oz) bunch of coriander, stalks and leaves

1. Put all the ingredients except the coriander into a saucepan. Chop the coriander stalks off the bunch, keeping them tied together so that you can fish them out later (reserve the leaves to garnish your dish), and add to the pan. Bring to the boil, then reduce the heat and simmer for 10 minutes while you prepare any additional ingredients.
2. After the broth has simmered for 10 minutes, strain into a jug, discarding the solids, and return to the saucepan. Bring the broth back to the boil.

sauces

Green onion & sesame sauce

From plain noodles to rice and grains as well as grilled salmon, this versatile sauce tastes great with almost everything. Add it to stir-fries to give them a flavour boost.

Serves 2
- 30 calories
- trace saturated fat

6 spring onions, roughly chopped
1 tbsp rice vinegar
1 tbsp soy sauce
1 tbsp mirin
1 tbsp toasted sesame oil
1 tbsp sesame paste or tahini

1. Put all the ingredients into a jug and whizz with a stick blender until smooth, or blend in a jug blender.

Spicy miso sauce

Stir this gutsy sauce into soups, or use as a salad dressing for an extra kick.

Serves 2
- 78 calories
- 0.9g saturated fat

1 tbsp toasted sesame oil
1 tbsp miso paste
2 tsp rice vinegar
1 tsp agave syrup
1 tsp garlic paste
½ tsp Chinese five-spice powder
1 hot red chilli, roughly chopped

1. Put all the ingredients into a jug and whizz to a smooth paste with a stick blender.

Peanut sauce

It is worth making extra of this delicious sauce, as it keeps well in the fridge for up to five days and can be used to dress salads and stir-fries as well as steamed vegetables and grilled chicken.

Serves 4
➕ 204 calories
🖤 8.4g saturated fat

80g (2¾oz) smooth peanut butter
1 tsp garlic paste
1 tsp ginger paste
1 hot green chilli, finely chopped
    (leave the seeds in for extra heat)
1 tbsp soy sauce
40g (1½oz) creamed coconut,
    dissolved in 4 tbsp hot water
2 tsp tamarind paste
1 tsp fish sauce
juice of 1 lime

1. Put all the ingredients into a blender and whizz to a sauce, or put into a jug and blend with a stick blender.

Stir-fry sauce

This classic sauce will enhance any stir-fry but tastes especially great with pork or duck.

Serves 2
➕ 45 calories
🖤 0.1g saturated fat

1 tbsp hoisin sauce
1 tbsp oyster sauce
1 tbsp soy sauce
2 hot red chillies, chopped
10g (¼oz) peeled and grated fresh
    root ginger or about ½ tbsp
    ginger paste

1. Put all the ingredients into a bowl and mix together well.

Dressing for grains

Bring masses of flavour to whole grains by adding this delicious dressing. Then mix with vegetables or cooked chicken to make healthy, filling salads.

Serves 2
➕ 70 calories
⬇ 0.4g saturated fat

1 tbsp miso paste
1 tbsp maple syrup or clear honey
1 tbsp rice vinegar
1 tbsp itsu Hot•su Potsu Sauce, Sriracha chilli sauce or other hot red chilli sauce
1 tbsp soy sauce
1 tsp toasted sesame oil

1. Put all the ingredients into a bowl and mix together well.

Thai salad dressing

This is a dressing to make all manner of Asian-style salads sing with flavour.

Serves 2
➕ 97 calories
⬇ 0.4g saturated fat

4 tbsp lime juice
2 tbsp fish sauce
1–2 hot red chillies, chopped
1 tbsp agave syrup
1 garlic clove, finely chopped or crushed, or 1 tsp garlic paste
1 tbsp rapeseed oil

1. Put all the ingredients into a bowl and mix together well.

Ginger teriyaki sauce

itsu's take on the classic Japanese sauce, the addition of fresh ginger gives it added zing. Use this sauce to glaze salmon or chicken, or to dress vegetables.

Serves 2

- 83 calories
- 1.3g saturated fat

1 tbsp groundnut oil
1 shallot, diced
10g (¼oz) peeled fresh root ginger, sliced
1 tsp cornflour or potato flour
100ml (3½fl oz) water
3 tbsp teriyaki sauce
1 tbsp soy sauce
½ tsp black pepper

1. Heat the oil in a small saucepan and fry the shallot and ginger over a medium heat for 1 minute.
2. Put the cornflour or potato flour in a cup or small bowl and mix with a tablespoon of water to a smooth paste, then add to the shallot and ginger along with the measured water, the teriyaki and soy sauces and black pepper.
3. Bring to the boil, stirring as the sauce starts to bubble and thicken, and cook for 1 minute, then remove from the heat.

Asian pesto

This super-green sauce brings colour and herb-fresh flavour to any hot or cold dish. Stir through grains, pour over cooked chicken or fish or use it to dress noodles.

Serves 2

- 100 calories
- 0.9g saturated fat

50g (1¾oz) bunch of coriander, stalks and leaves
1 tbsp mint leaves
1 hot red chilli, seeds in, roughly chopped
a thumb-sized piece of fresh root ginger (about 20g/¾oz), peeled
1 garlic clove, peeled
1 tbsp toasted sesame oil
1 tbsp soy sauce
¼ tsp salt
1 tbsp lemon or lime juice
1 tbsp agave syrup

1. Hold the bunch of coriander under the tap to rinse, then shake it to remove most of the water. Roughly chop, including the stalks, and put it into a blender with mint and chilli.
2. Grate the ginger and garlic and add to the coriander in the blender, along with the remaining ingredients, and blend to a sauce.

Spicy udon sauce

This spicy, fragrant sauce is ideal stirred into cooked udon noodles or tossed with vegetables to add some extra heat.

Serves 2
- 60 calories
- 0.4g saturated fat

4 tbsp itsu Hot•su Potsu Sauce, Sriracha chilli sauce or other hot red chilli sauce
2 tbsp soy sauce
2 tsp rice vinegar
juice of ½ lime
½ tbsp toasted sesame oil
1 tbsp chopped chives
1 tbsp chopped coriander

1. Put all the ingredients into a bowl and mix together well.

Variation: if you can't find chives, substitute the finely chopped green tops of spring onions, or use 1 tsp garlic paste instead.

Walnut miso

This can also be used as a dressing for cooked chicken or steamed vegetables to serve with rice.

Serves 2
- 186 calories
- 1.4g saturated fat

50g (1¾oz) ground walnuts
1 tbsp miso paste
2 tsp rice vinegar
1 tbsp soy sauce
1 tsp agave syrup or any brown sugar
1 tbsp water

1. Put all the walnut miso ingredients into a jug and whizz to a smooth paste with a stick blender.

Red coconut curry sauce

'Pimp up' ready-made red curry paste to create an invigorating sauce for Potsus (*see* page 93), chicken or just plain rice and vegetables.

Serves 2
- 213 calories
- 12.9g saturated fat

4 tbsp Thai red curry paste
160ml (5½fl oz) canned coconut milk
10g (¼oz) fresh root ginger, peeled
    and chopped
1 tbsp fish sauce
1 tsp agave syrup
1 tsp cornflour or potato flour
100ml (3½fl oz) water

1. Mix the curry paste, coconut milk, ginger, fish sauce and agave syrup together in a small saucepan.
2. Put the cornflour or potato flour in a cup or small bowl and mix with a tablespoon of water to a smooth paste, then add to the curry sauce along with the measured water and bring to the boil, stirring as it starts to bubble and thicken. Serve hot.

Sesame sauce

This is a great dressing for cold noodle salads. Buckwheat (soba) and somen noodles taste particularly good when paired with the nutty flavour of the sesame.

Serves 2
- 132 calories
- 1.5g saturated fat

2 tbsp sesame paste or tahini
a thumb-sized piece of fresh root
    ginger (about 20g/¾oz), peeled
    and grated
2 tbsp water
1 tbsp rice vinegar
1 tbsp soy sauce
1 tsp agave syrup

1. Put all the ingredients into a bowl and mix together well.

Index